No PhDs Please: This is Canada

Dismal Employment and Earning Prospects of PhDs in an Advanced Resource Rich Country

MAHMOOD IQBAL, *PhD*

Dedication

To all those *with* a PhD who have to drive taxies, deliver pizzas and perform similar tasks to sustain their livelihood.

Contents

Acknowledgement

Thanks to Dr. Munir Sheikh, Dr. Asif Chida, Dr. Arun Kumar and Mr. Michael Grant for their critique and valuable suggestions. Special thanks to my wife, Bushra for editing the book.

Introduction

"Doctorate recipients begin careers in large and small organizations, teach in universities, and start new businesses. Doctoral education develops human resources that are critical to a nation's progress— scientists, engineers, researchers, and scholars who create and share new knowledge and new ways of thinking that lead, directly and indirectly, to innovative products, services, and works of art. In doing so, they contribute to the economic growth, cultural development, and rising standard of living of a nation."

National Science Foundation (2009) <u>Doctorate Recipients from U.S. Universities</u> <u>http://www.nsf.gov/statistics/nsf11306/important.cfm</u>

This book will dispel the conventional wisdom that the highest possible education is always rewarded in all advanced economies. At least in the immediate future, this does not hold true for Canada. Due to its large dependence on resource sectors and its industrial structure the need for the PhDs (Philosophy of Doctorates) is very limited.

In spite of about six additional years of education, Canada's PhDs earn about the same as those who hold a Master's degree. Their prospects of finding employment are even worse. This book examines the value of a PhD in Canada from a broad perspective and is written in a format suitable for a wide audience: professionals, business executives, governments and policy makers.

Importance

In an increasingly knowledge-driven, innovative and global economy, importance of higher education can hardly be emphasized. It increases research capability, teaching, training and learning opportunities, which are necessary ingredients for today's economic competitiveness and higher productivity. It generates higher life-time earnings, more secured employability and more flexibility to changing market conditions. Overall returns to society are even larger because many benefits of education are not pecuniary.

However, economic returns and employment situation of higher educated persons in Canada — as compared to U.S. and other OECD countries — are disturbing. On average, PhDs take six more years after

Masters to complete the program. However, PhDs earn only 8% higher than Masters in Canada[1] (as compared to 22% higher in U.S.[2]). Their unemployment rate, bafflingly, is 50% higher than Masters in Canada (while it is just the opposite in U.S., 36% lower). A recent government survey shows that 200 (out of 50,101) taxi drivers in Canada are doctors or PhDs.[3]

The objective of this book is to examine the state of PhDs vis-à-vis university graduates in Canada; their earnings and employment situation. To investigate reasons for their poor earning and employment prospects compared to their counterparts in U.S. (and OECD) in broader economic perspectives. Resource richness, traditional industrial structure, lack of innovative opportunities and primary commodity focused production and trade pattern in Canada may be factors deterring enhanced prospects of PhDs in the country.

How is this book different?

This book will consolidate the data and analyses related to the economic opportunities of PhDs in Canada and present them basically through self-explanatory charts.

- Existing reports are highly technical. The data is also scattered.

- Many reports lump Bachelors,Masters and PhDs together in one category: "university graduates." Only a few reports focus on economic opportunities for PhDs in Canada, and presentation is very technical.

- Studies rarely compare the state of PhDs in Canada with the competing countries — United States and OECD (Organization of Economic Cooperation and Development).

- None of the reports investigates reasons for dismal economic prospects of PhDs in Canada.

It is important to highlight at the outset that due to severe and continued budget cuts, Statistics Canada could not conduct *Doctoral Surveys* and similar research on regular basis — main source

1   Statistics Canada (2009) *Graduating in Canada: Profile, Labour Market Outcomes and Student Debt of the Class of 2005* by Justin Bayard and Edith Greenlee, Catalogue no. 81-595-M –No. 074.

2   U.S. Bureau of Labor Statistics (2010) Current Population Survey http://www.bls.gov/emp/ep_chart_001.htm

3   *The Globe and Mail* (May 10, 2012) "Overqualified immigrants really are driving taxis in Canada" http://www.theglobeandmail.com/commentary/editorials/overqualified-immigrants-really-are-driving-taxis-in-canada/article4106352/

for employment and income data of Canadian PhDs. This forced the present study to rely on out-dated data. However, keeping in view Canada's economic environment (increased production in number of university graduates and PhDs, budget cuts of institutions and departments who tend to hire PhDs, significant drop in full time academic positions, especially tenured) and global reality (increased demand for Canada's oil, gas, forest and natural resources from emerging economies of Asia — industries which seldom need highly educated and R&D personals), one can safely specu-late that job prospects, earning and growth opportunities of post graduate degree holders, especial-ly of PhDs might have deteriorated over the years. Past data confirm similar trends.

The study examines only monetary benefit of PhDs. It does not consider non-pecuniary and social benefits of higher education. Also it ignores the psychological toll of being unemployed and lower pay even after highest education.

Chapter I: Doctoral Graduates

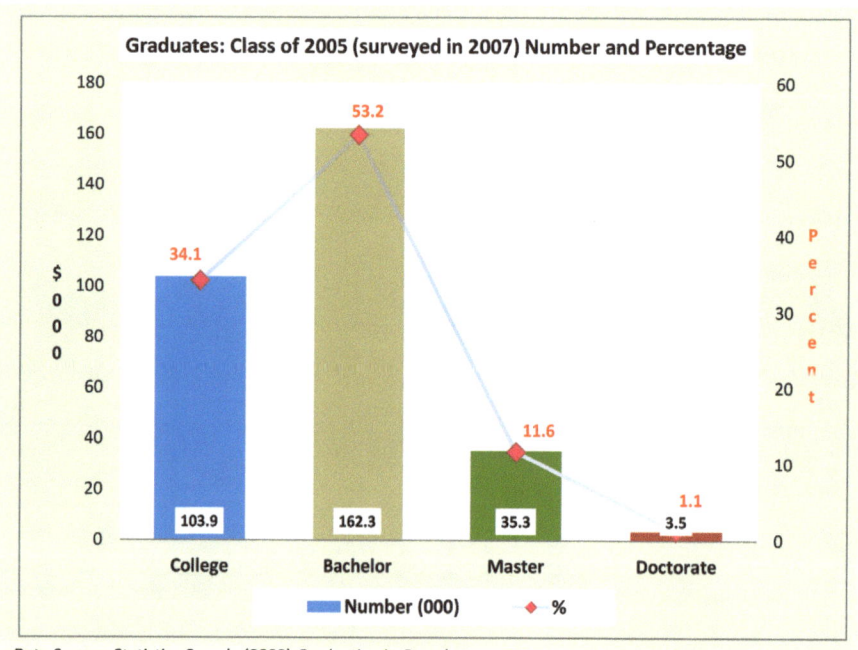

Data Source: Statistics Canada (2009) *Graduating in Canada.*

According to a survey conducted in 2009 by Statistics Canada of 305,000 students who graduated from colleges and Universities in 2005 (the latest data available), only 1.1% were PhDs and 11.6% were Masters (*Chart I.1*).

Chart I.2

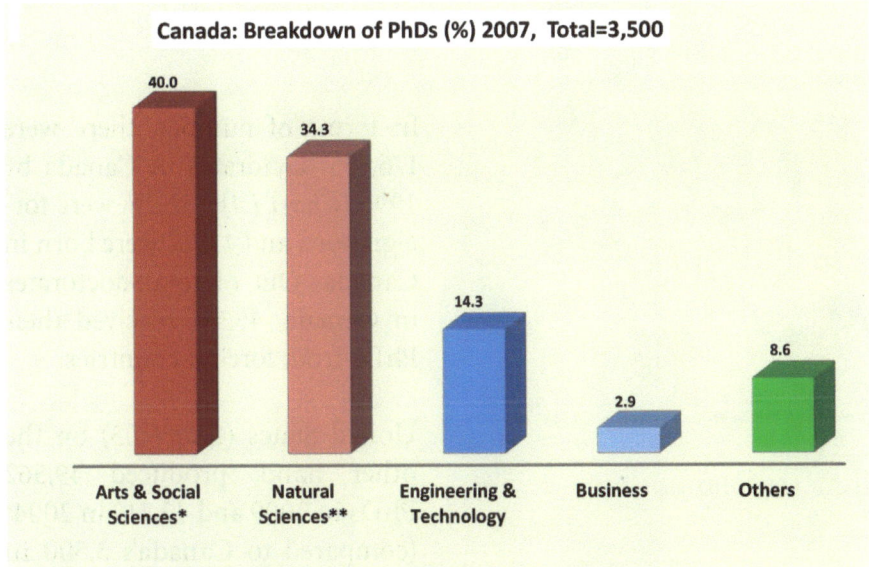

Out of 3,500 PhDs produced in 2007 (*Chart I.2*), 40% were in arts and social sciences, 34.3% in natural sciences, 14.3% in engineering, 2.9% in business and 8.6% in other disciplines.[1]

Arts & Social Sciences* = Education, visual arts, humanities and social sciences.
Natural Sciences** = Physical, life sciences, mathematics, computer, agriculture & natural resources
Others = Health, fitness & other services.
Data Source: Statistics Canada (2009) *Graduating in Canada.*

Chart I.3

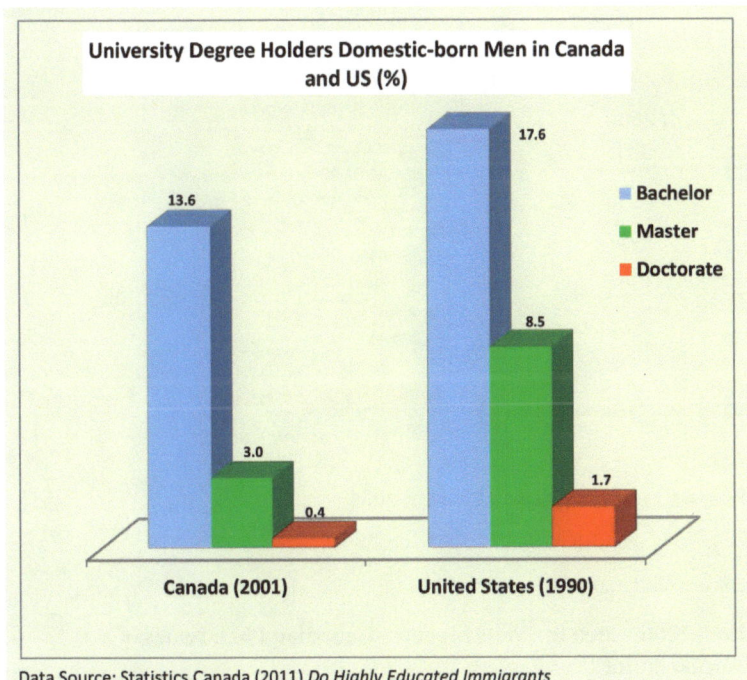

Another study[2] comparing Canada with the United States only for men and domestic born (*Chart I.3*) shows that proportion of university degree holders at all education level are higher in U.S.: 8.5% Master in U.S. compared to 3% in Canada and 1.7% PhDs in U.S. compared to only 0.4% in Canada. Note: U.S. data lag behind by 10-year. Number would be even higher for U.S. for the year 2001.

Data Source: Statistics Canada (2011) *Do Highly Educated Immigrants*

1   Data Source: Statistics Canada (2009) *Graduating in Canada: Profile, Labour Market Outcomes and Student Debt of the Class of 2005* by Justin Bayard and Edith Greenlee, Catalogue no. 81-595-M — No. 074.
2   Statistics Canada (2011) *Do Highly Educated Immigrants Perform Differently In the Canadian and U.S. Labour Markets?* by Bonikowska, Feng Hou, and Garnett Picot.

Chart I.4

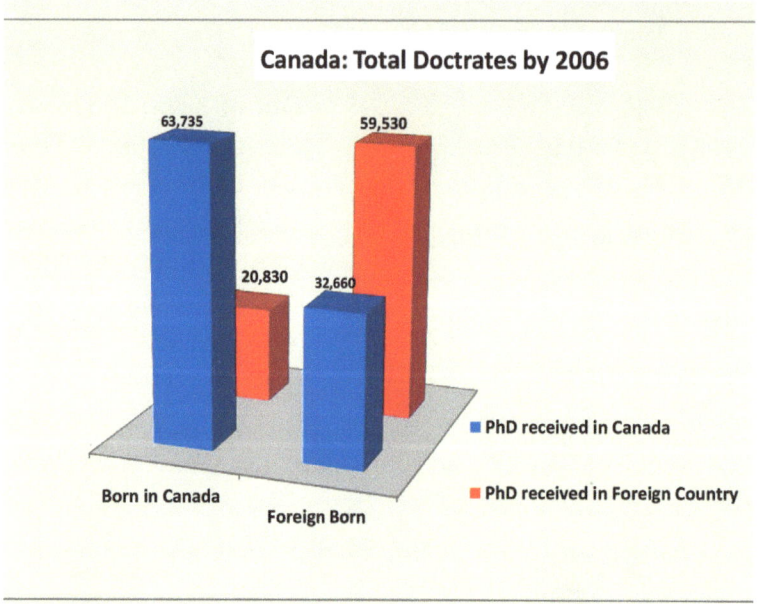

Data Sources: Statistics Canada, *Census of Population*, 2006 and OECD, 2007.

In terms of number, there were 176,755 doctorates in Canada by 1996 (*Chart I.4*)[3]: 52.2% were foreign born and 47.7% were born in Canada. Out of total doctorates in Canada, 45.5% received their PhDs from foreign countries.

United States (*Chart I.5*) on the other hand, produced 49,562 PhDs in 2009 and 42,118 in 2004[4] (compared to Canada's 3,500 in 2005). In 2009, 45% were in social sciences, humanities and other disciplines, 23% in life sciences, 17% in physical sciences and 15% in Engineering.

Chart I.5

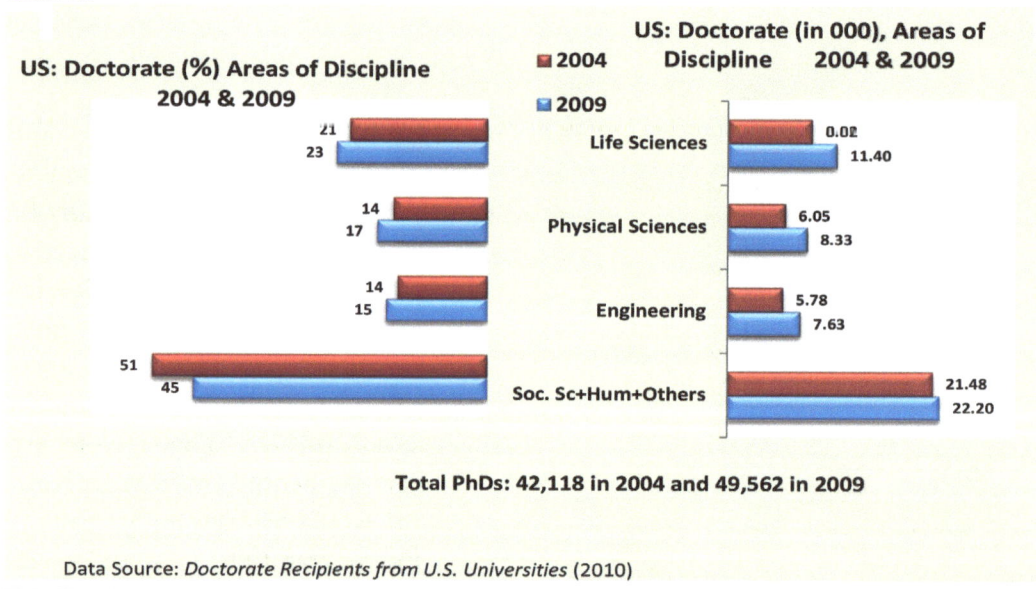

Data Source: *Doctorate Recipients from U.S. Universities* (2010)

---

3   Statistics Canada, *Census of Population*, 2006. Cited by Louis Maheu: "Canadian PhD: Issues of a 'Building' Strategy", *The Canadian Review of Sociology*, for Peer Review.

4   National Science Foundation (2010) *Doctorate Recipients from U.S. Universities: 2009* (NSF 11-306).

Note: U.S. has 9 times higher population than Canada, but it produced 14 times more PhDs. Moreover, only 1.9% of its PhDs were unemployed as compared to 6% in Canada (shown in the next section). This implies that U.S. economy has far more absorptive capacity, employment and research opportunities for its PhDs than Canada. Translated in Canadian equivalent, unemployment rate of U.S. PhDs should have been 8.4% (=6% x 1.4) even after adjusting for U.S. 9 times larger size of the economy, and not its existing unemployment rate of only 1.9%.

Chart I.6

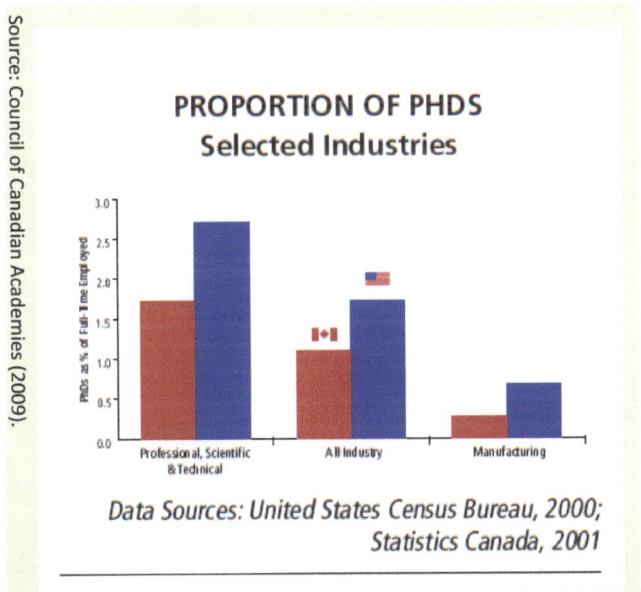

PROPORTION OF PHDS
Selected Industries

Data Sources: United States Census Bureau, 2000;
Statistics Canada, 2001

PhDs employed in various industries (*Chart I.6*) is significantly higher in U.S., especially in professional, scientific and technical field; where the proportion is as high as 60%.

Chart I.7

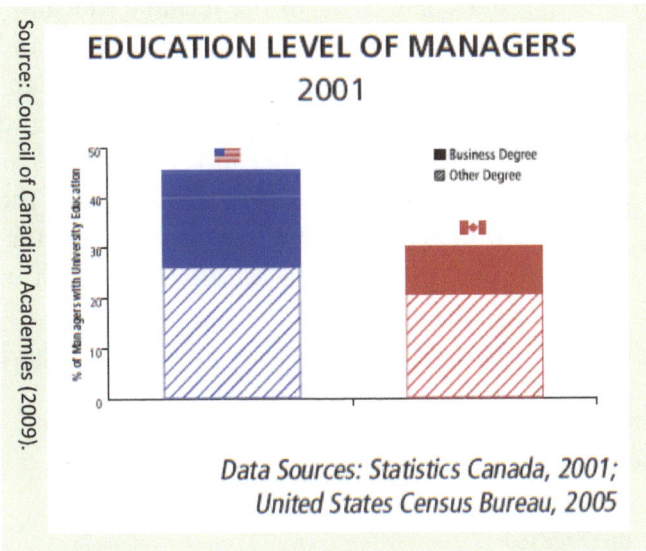

EDUCATION LEVEL OF MANAGERS
2001

Business Degree
Other Degree

Data Sources: Statistics Canada, 2001;
United States Census Bureau, 2005

The same is true with the number of managers with university degrees (Chart *I.7*): the percentage is 46% in U.S. as compared to 30% in Canada. Further, more managers hold business degrees in U.S.

Chart I.8

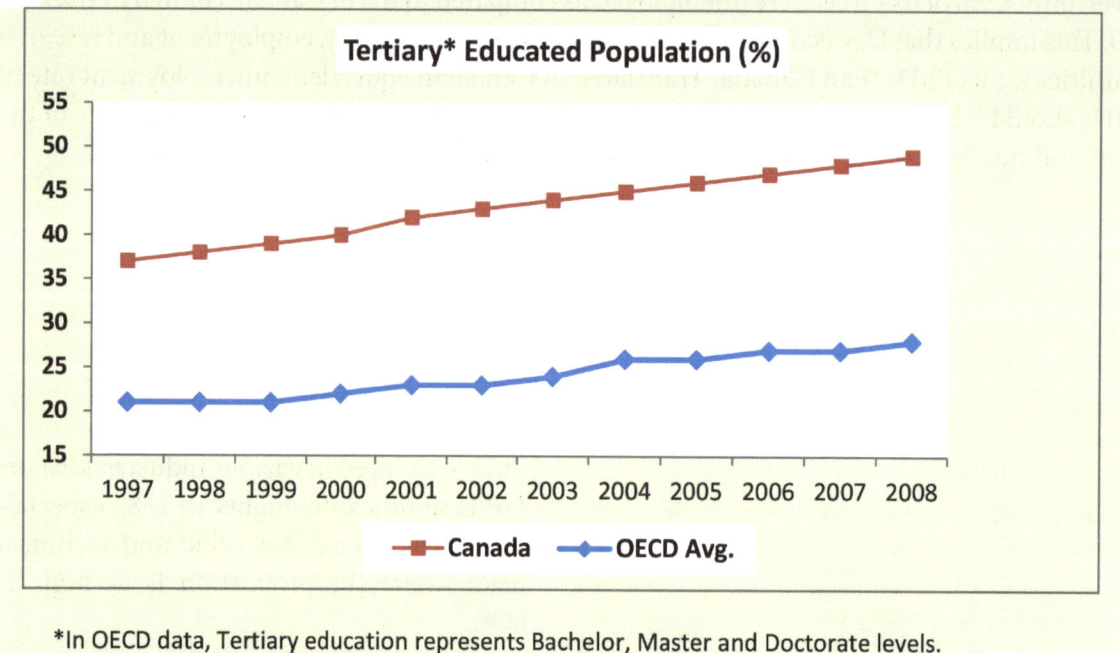

*In OECD data, Tertiary education represents Bachelor, Master and Doctorate levels.
Data Source: *Education at a Glance, OECD Indicators*, 2010

Chart I.9

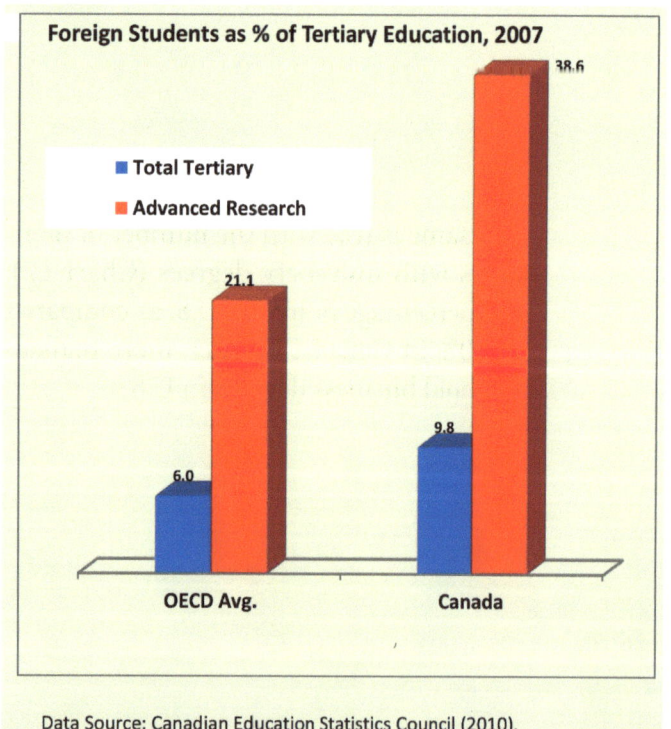

A bigger picture can be seen in OECD data. The trend in the tertiary education which includes Bachelors, Masters and Doctorates, is quite positive in both Canada and OECD countries (*Chart I.8*), and proportion is higher in Canada (9.8% as compared to 6% in OECD). However, the proportion of foreign student doctorates (measured by advanced research in OECD data) is quite significant in Canada: 83% higher than the OECD (*Chart I.9*).

Data Source: Canadian Education Statistics Council (2010).

Chapter II: Higher Education and Economic Return

Higher degrees in humanities should carry a warning: "Earning this degree, while intellectually stimulating, may increase your chances of life long poverty and disillusionment."
A comment, *The New York Times.* http://www.nytimes.com/2011/05/27/opinion/ l27jobs.html?ref=opinion

Chart II:1

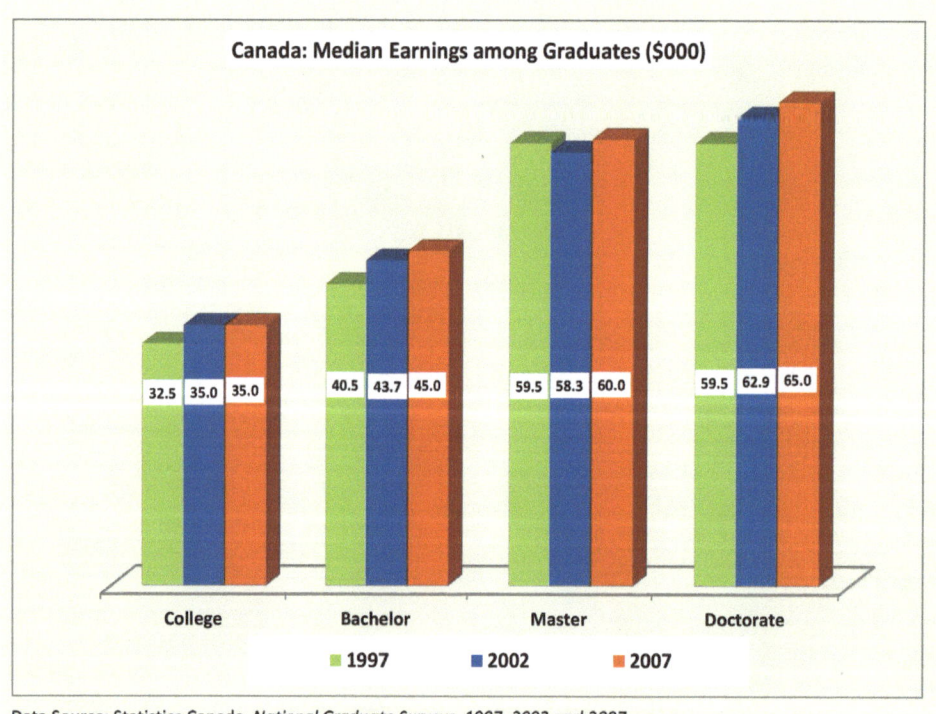

Canada: Median Earnings among Graduates ($000)

College: 32.5 | 35.0 | 35.0
Bachelor: 40.5 | 43.7 | 45.0
Master: 59.5 | 58.3 | 60.0
Doctorate: 59.5 | 62.9 | 65.0

■ 1997 ■ 2002 ■ 2007

Data Source: Statistics Canada, *National Graduate Surveys, 1997, 2002 and 2007.*

Median earnings of all level of graduates remained pretty stable over the years in Canada (*Chart II.1*). There is not much difference in the earnings of Doctorates as compared to Masters. For example, PhDs earned 8% more than Masters in 2007 even after 5-6 years of more schooling.

Chart II.2

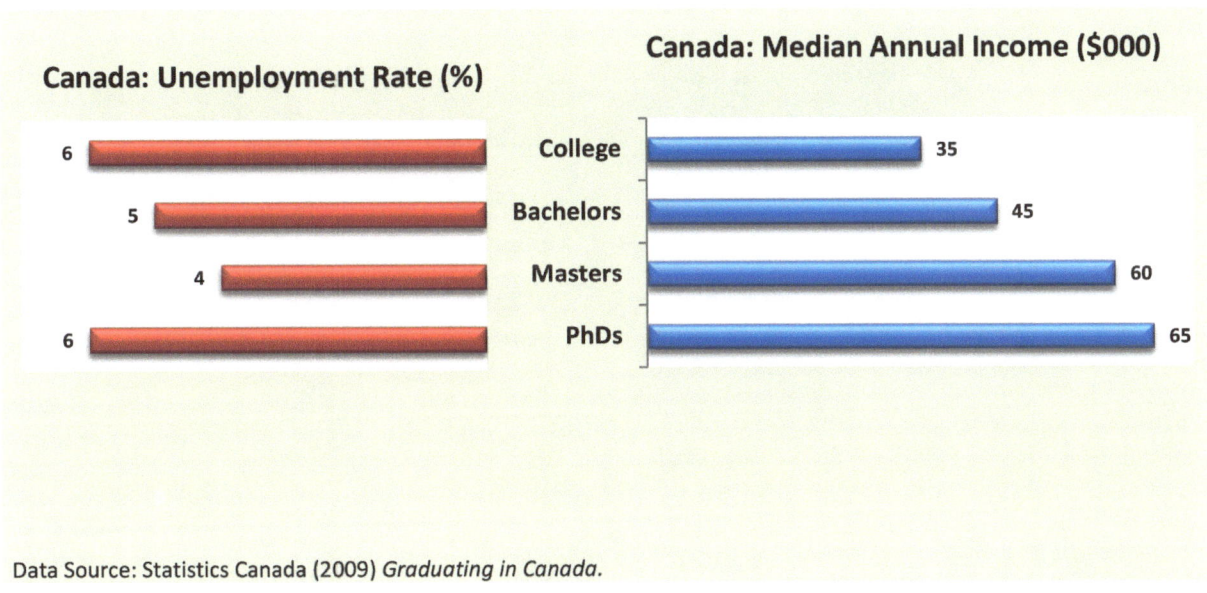

Canada: Unemployment Rate (%) | Canada: Median Annual Income ($000)

	Unemployment Rate (%)	Median Annual Income ($000)
College	6	35
Bachelors	5	45
Masters	4	60
PhDs	6	65

Data Source: Statistics Canada (2009) *Graduating in Canada.*

The other striking thing is that the unemployment rate for PhDs is 50% higher than Masters (*Chart II.2*).

Even for professional class (lawyers and medical doctors), situation is not rosy. According to a *Globe and Mail* article,[1] young professionals are facing a painful double squeeze: significant increase in tuitions (for example, $25,000 per year in the law school and competition is ferocious to get in), while income prospects are far lower than the expected $100,000 after completing a law degree. Further, three years of undergraduate work in law is not sufficient. By the time a law degree is completed, one may have a debt of $80,000 or more.

Similarly, by the time a student qualifies as a medical doctor, she is already into her 30s with $180,000 in debt. And she has only one client to sell her service — government — whose ability and willingness to pay is shrinking fast.

According to a survey conducted by the Canadian Association of Postdoctoral Scholars in 2009,[2] there were about 6,000 postdocs: 80 percent earned $45,000 or less a year before taxes. They had few job benefits and little chance of finding permanent employment as faculty members.

---

[1]   The Globe and Mail (April 28, 2012) "The professional-class bubble is bursting" by Margaret Wente http://www.theglobeandmail.com/commentary/the-professional-class-bubble-is-bursting/article4103298

[2]   Cited in *University Affairs* (January 11, 2010) by Rosanna Tamburri. http://www.universityaffairs.ca/give-us-the-dirt-on-jobs.aspx

Chart II.3

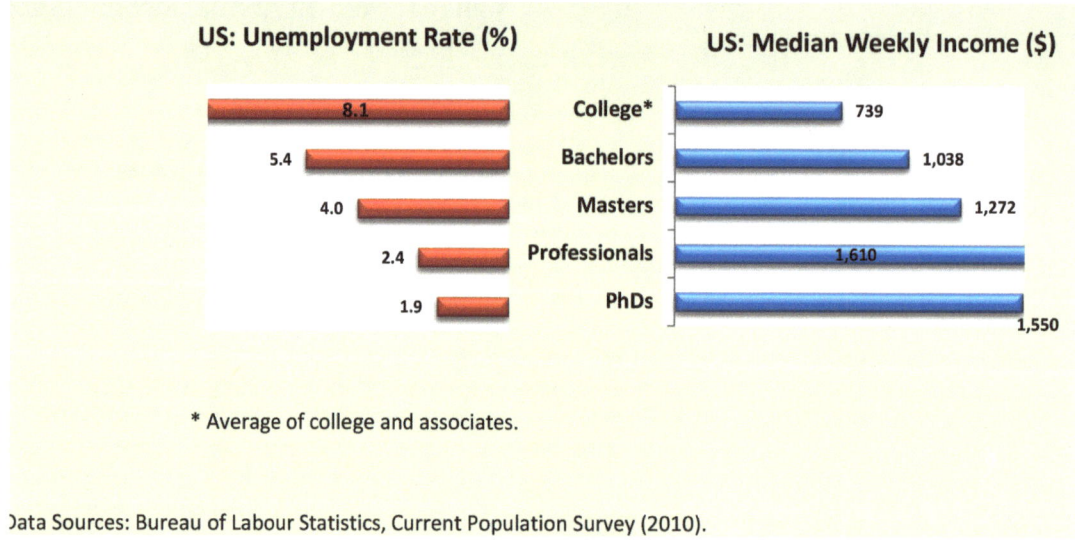

US: Unemployment Rate (%)   US: Median Weekly Income ($)

	Unemployment Rate (%)	Median Weekly Income ($)
College*	8.1	739
Bachelors	5.4	1,038
Masters	4.0	1,272
Professionals	2.4	1,610
PhDs	1.9	1,550

* Average of college and associates.

Data Sources: Bureau of Labour Statistics, Current Population Survey (2010).

Chart II.4

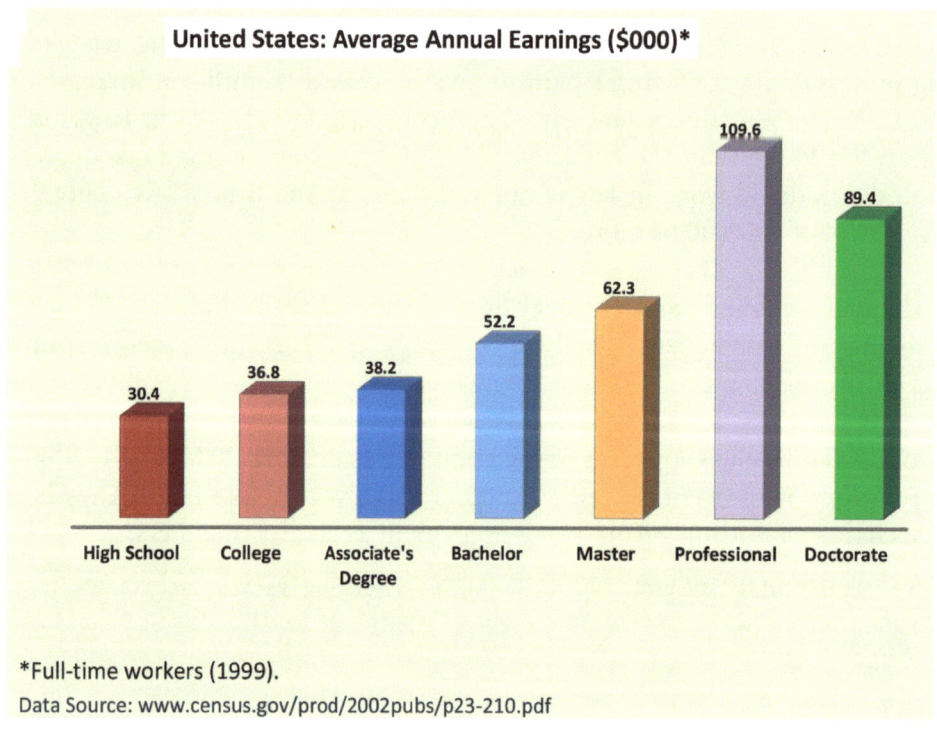

United States: Average Annual Earnings ($000)*

High School	College	Associate's Degree	Bachelor	Master	Professional	Doctorate
30.4	36.8	38.2	52.2	62.3	109.6	89.4

*Full-time workers (1999).
Data Source: www.census.gov/prod/2002pubs/p23-210.pdf

In the United States, picture is just the opposite (*Chart II.3*). The unemployment rate of PhDs, as compared to Masters is 52% lower: 1.9% versus 4%. At the same time, income of PhDs, as compared to Masters is 22% higher, based on weekly earnings; and 43% higher based on annual earnings (*Chart II.4*). Professionals, on average, earn as high as $110,000 a year.

Chart II.5

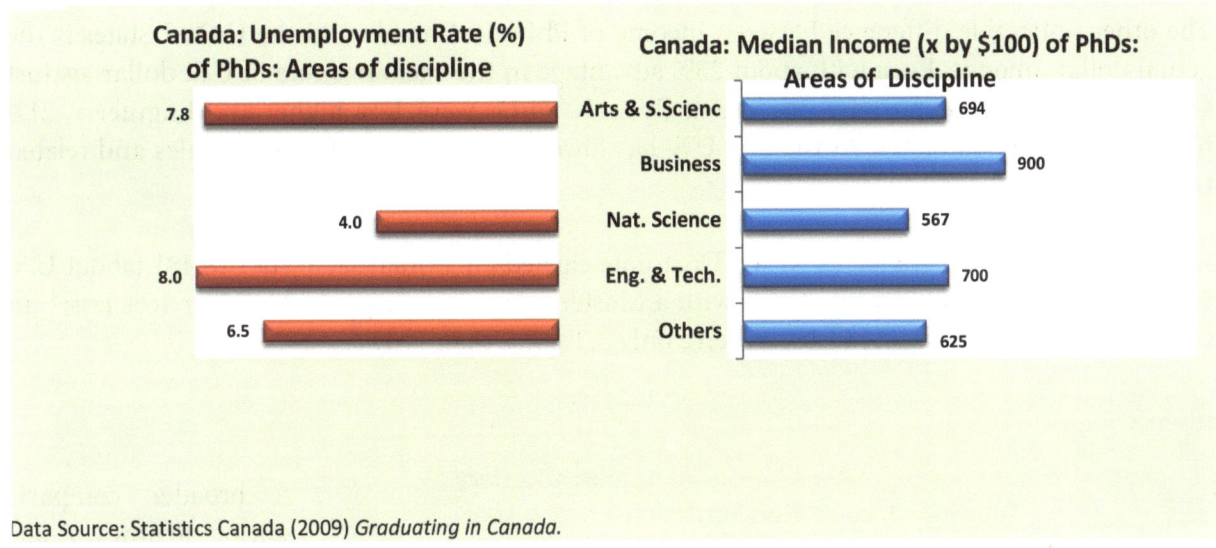

Data Source: Statistics Canada (2009) *Graduating in Canada.*

A breakdown of income and unemployment of PhDs in Canada by disciplines (*Chart II.5*) shows that PhDs in Business earn the highest ($90,000 a year), followed by Engineering and Technology. However, due to low R&D and employment opportunities for highly specialized personals in technology fields in Canada, unemployment rate of Engineering PhDs is the highest: 8%; even higher than PhDs in arts and social sciences. (Unemployment rate in Business area is not available.)

Chart II.6

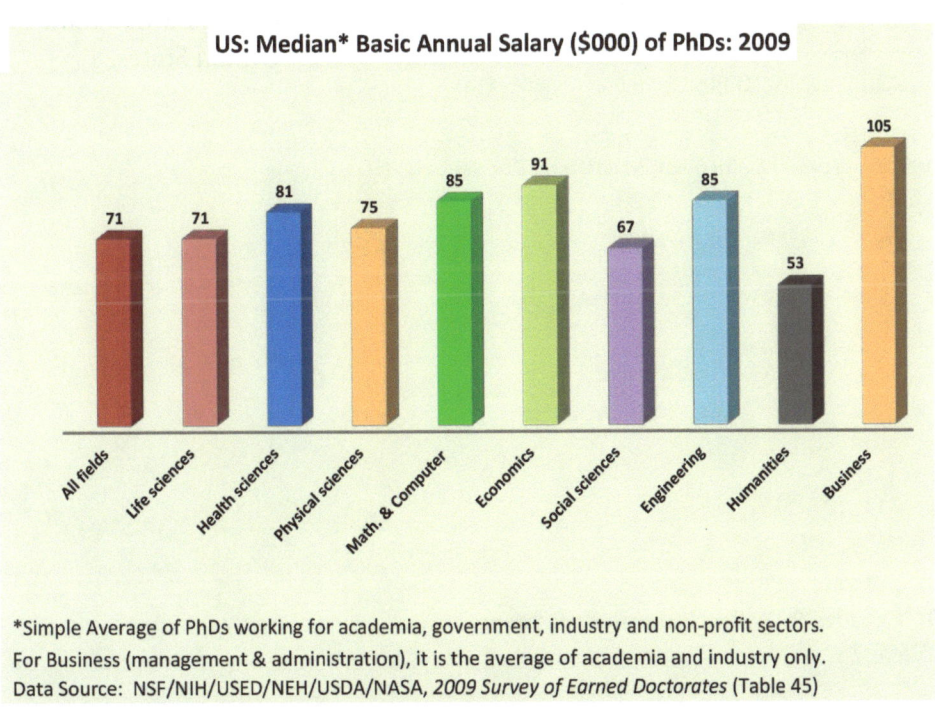

*Simple Average of PhDs working for academia, government, industry and non-profit sectors.
For Business (management & administration), it is the average of academia and industry only.
Data Source: NSF/NIH/USED/NEH/USDA/NASA, *2009 Survey of Earned Doctorates* (Table 45)

Same holds true about the income of PhDs in the United States (*Chart II.6*). Business graduates earn the highest, followed by PhDs in Economics. Engineering and Computer Science PhDs are next in the pack.

The other noticeable difference between income of PhDs in Canada and the United States is the actual dollar amount. Even with about 25% advantage in the exchange rate of U.S. dollar against Can$ (the period under study), income of Business PhDs were 17% higher and Engineers, 21% higher in the United States. At the top, U.S. has lower overall personal income, sales and related taxes.

In Britain in 2006-07, graduates with a Doctorate earned an annual salary of £28,481 (about U.S. $55,800 on January 2007) while those with a Master's degree were paid £23,832 or 16% less;[3] (in Canada, on the other hand, Masters receive only 3.2% less than PhDs).

Chart II.7

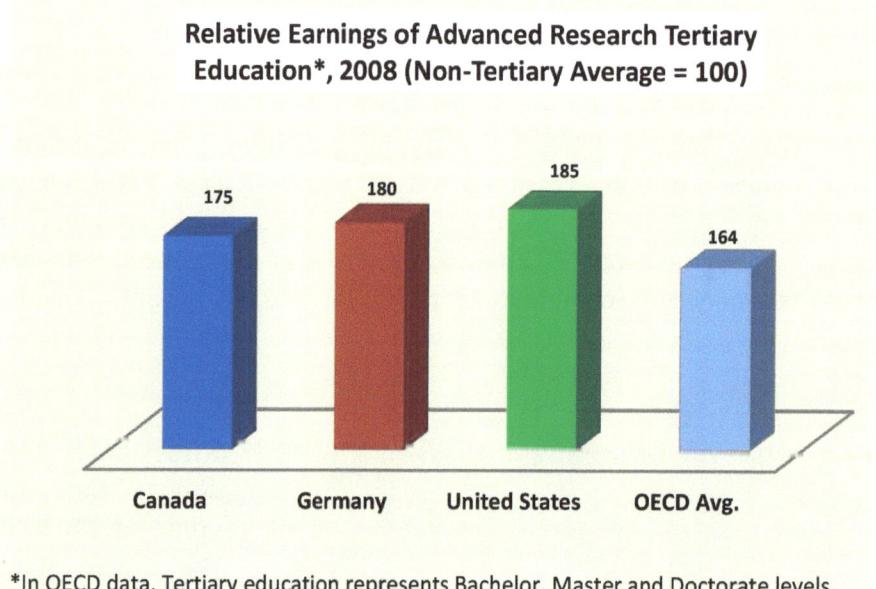

A broader comparison of earnings of advanced tertiary graduates (basically PhDs equivalent) in selected countries (*Chart II.7*) shows that Canada's position is above the OECD average, but 3% lower than Germany and 6% lower than the United States.

*In OECD data, Tertiary education represents Bachelor, Master and Doctorate levels.
Advanced research is PhD equivalent.
Data Source: *Education at a Glance, OECD Indicators*, 2010.

---

[3]   Philip Fine (2009) "Canada: PhD offers little salary difference" http://www.universityworldnews.com/article.php?story=20090521180150737

Chart II.8

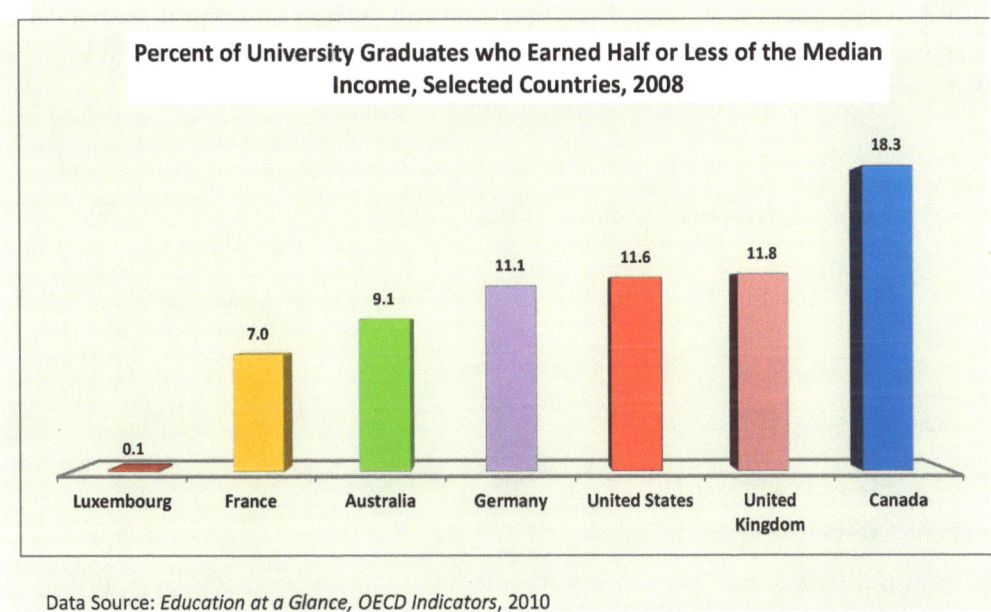

Percent of University Graduates who Earned Half or Less of the Median Income, Selected Countries, 2008

Data Source: *Education at a Glance, OECD Indicators*, 2010

Moreover, percentage of university graduates who earn half or less than the median income is significantly higher in Canada among the OECD countries (*Chart II.8*). For example, as compared to Canadian University graduates, there are 50% less Australian university graduates whose median income is half or less than the median income. Note that Australia is a resource rich country like Canada.

Chart II.9

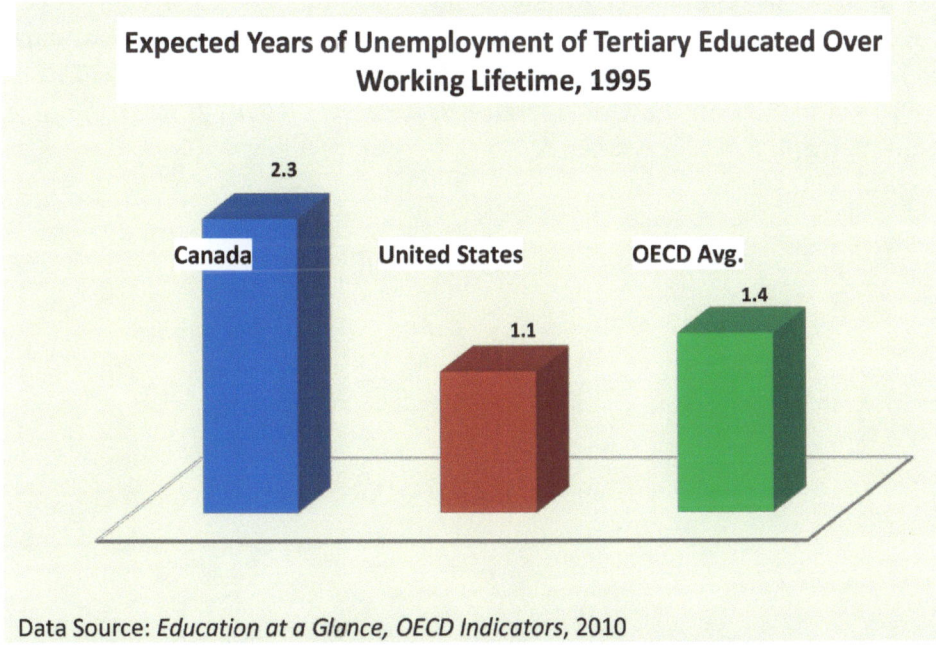

Expected Years of Unemployment of Tertiary Educated Over Working Lifetime, 1995

Data Source: *Education at a Glance, OECD Indicators*, 2010

The other negative fact for Canada is the expected number of years of unemployment of its tertiary educated graduates (that include Bachelors, Masters and PhDs). As compared to graduates in the United States (*Chart II.9*), Canadian graduates could experience 109% more unemployment over their lifetime. When compared with OECD average and expressed in other way: OECD graduates should expect 64% better prospect in keeping themselves employed over their working lifetime than Canadian graduates.

Chart II.10

Private Internal Rate of Return from Tertiary Education

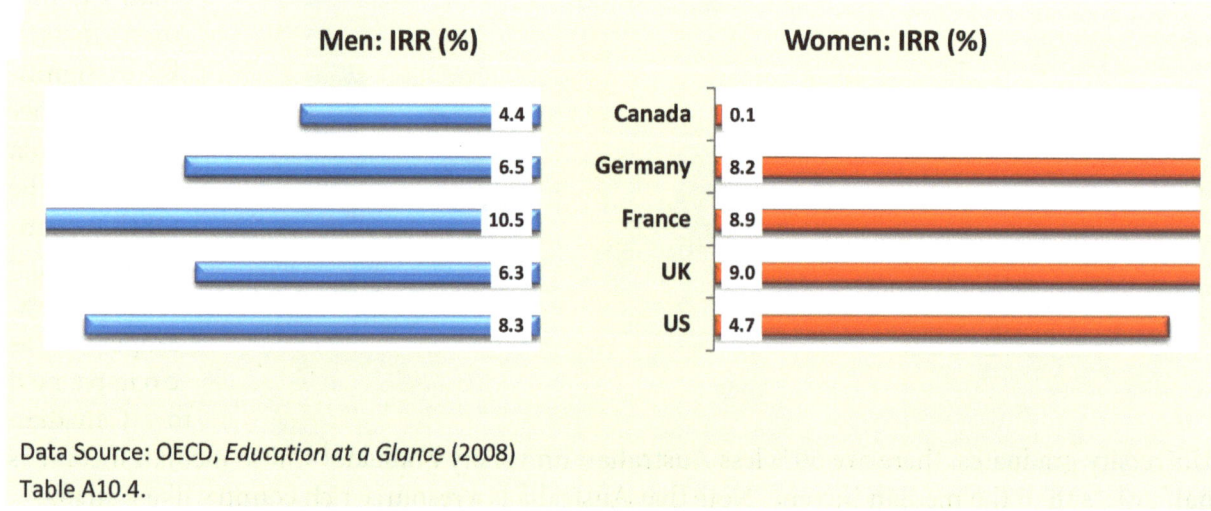

Data Source: OECD, *Education at a Glance* (2008)
Table A10.4.

The most comprehensive measure of economic worth of tertiary education is the private IRR (Internal Rate of Return). It takes into account the present and future earnings, adjusted with yearly cost and then expressed in present value term. For men, IRR is 4.4% and for women, only 0.1% in Canada as compared to 8.3% and 4.7% in the United States, respectively (*Chart II.10*). In France, IRR is as high as 10.5% for men and 8.9% for women.

Chart II.11

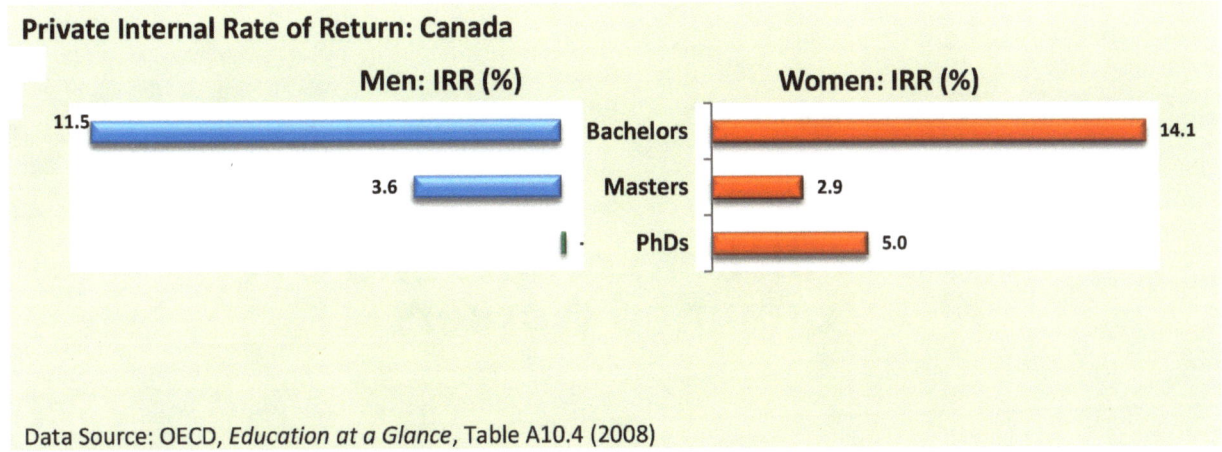

Data Source: OECD, *Education at a Glance*, Table A10.4 (2008)

A breakdown of IRR by degrees for Canada (*Charts II.11*)[4] shows that IRR for male PhDs is negative, while it is 3.6% for Masters and 11.5% for Bachelors. For women PhDs, IRR is not only significantly positive but also higher than Masters.

---

4   CD Howe Institute (2009) *Extra Earning Power: The Financial Returns to University Education in Canada* by Karim Mousaly-Sergieh and François Vaillancourt.

Chapter III: Immigrants and Over-qualified Workers

Chart III.1

Since 1990, the number of immigrants to Canada with graduate degrees has increased almost 5-fold

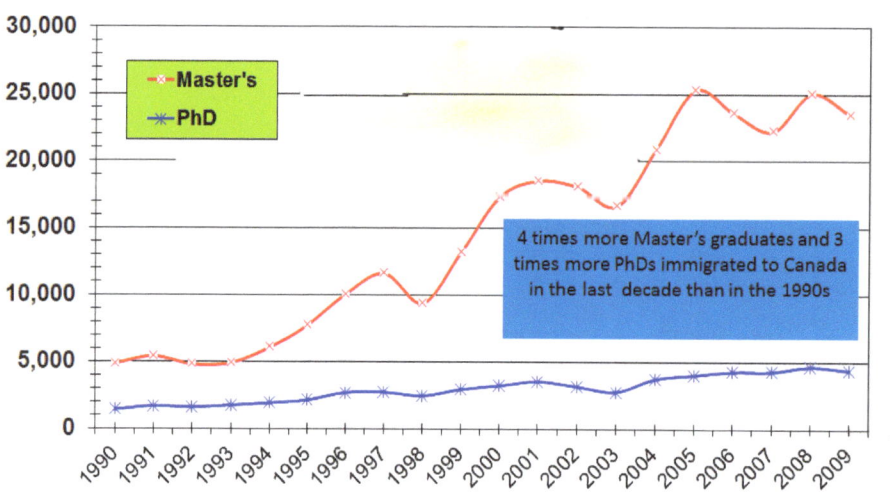

4 times more Master's graduates and 3 times more PhDs immigrated to Canada in the last decade than in the 1990s

Source: Statistics Canada, Citizenship and Immigration Canada

Since 1990, the number of immigrants to Canada with graduate degrees (Masters and PhDs) has increased almost five-fold (*Chart III.1*). More specifically, the number of immigrants coming to Canada with PhDs has grown from roughly 1,500 in 1990 to 4,600 in 2008.[1]

---

1   Cited in University Affairs (December 13, 2011) by Léo Charbonneau.

Chart III.2

University Educated Population in Canada

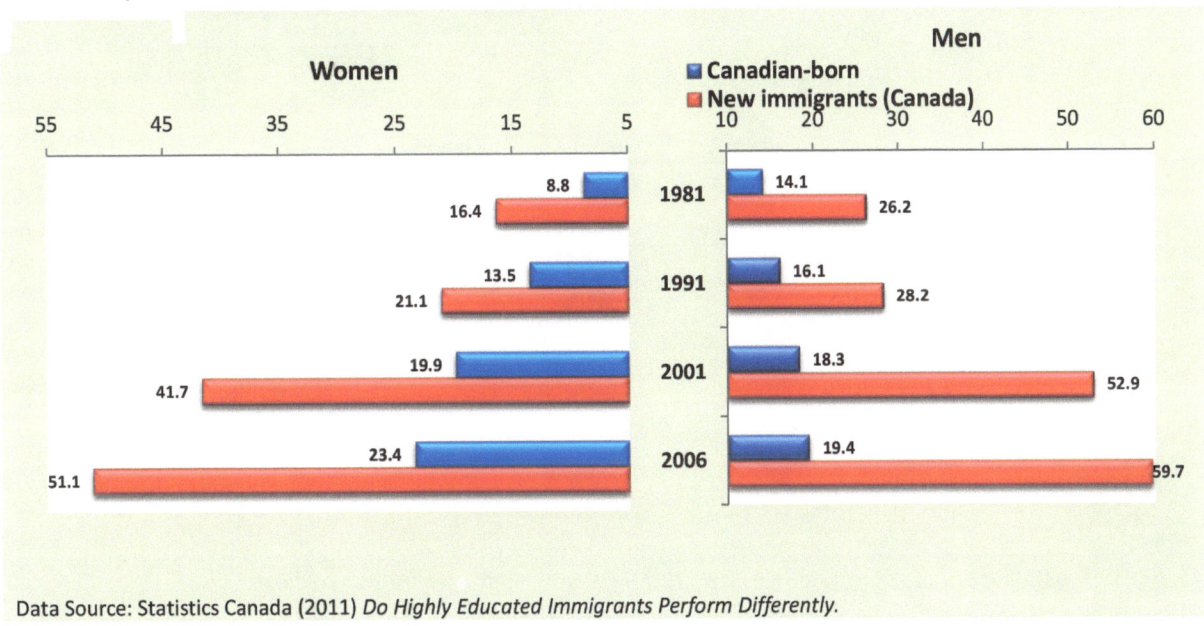

Data Source: Statistics Canada (2011) *Do Highly Educated Immigrants Perform Differently.*

A breakdown of university educated Canadian born and new immigrants (10 years or less) by gender (*Chart III.2*) shows that the proportion of immigrant university educated far exceeds Canadian born for both men and women.

This gap has continuously increased over decades. For example, 26.2% immigrant men and 16.4% immigrant women were university educated in 1981. This proportion increased to 59.7% for immigrant men and 51.1% for immigrant women in 2006. The gap (in favour of immigrants) was about 86% for both men and women in 1981, but increased to 207% for men and 118% for women in 2006. Note this gap between immigrants and Canadian born would be even higher when foreign students (or temporary visa holders) are included in the calculation.

Chart III.3

University Educated Population in U.S.

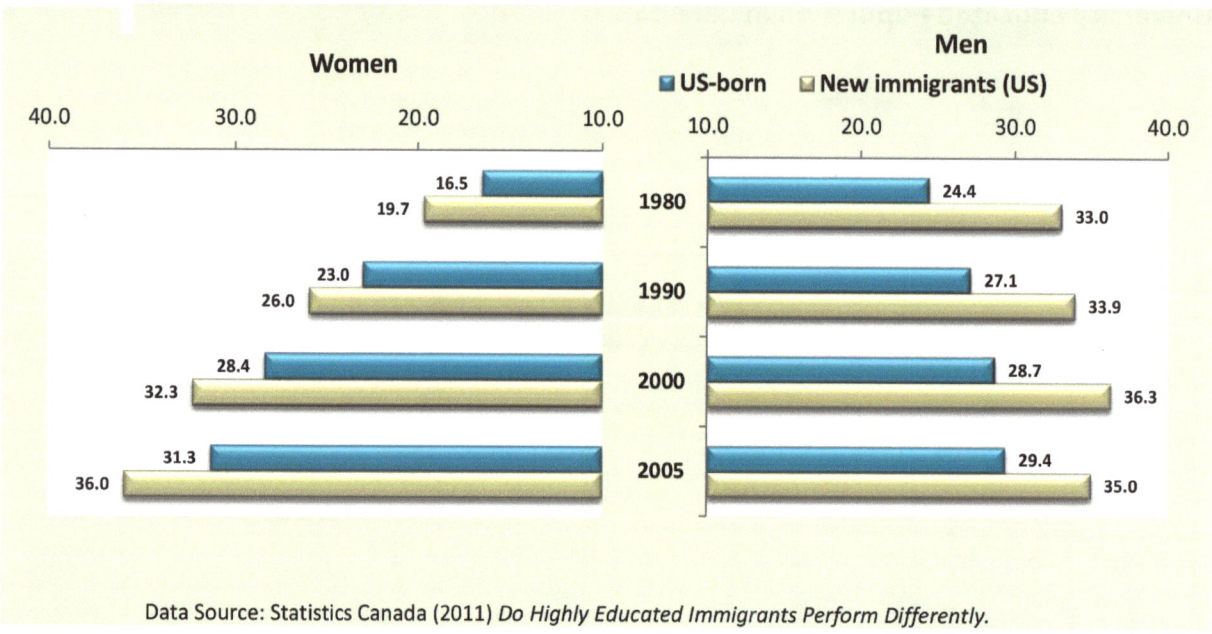

Data Source: Statistics Canada (2011) *Do Highly Educated Immigrants Perform Differently.*

The gap of university educated domestic born and new immigrants in the United States is hardly significant (*Chart III.3*). For example it was only 19% for men and 15% for women (in favor of immigrants) in the year 2005.

Moreover, unlike Canada, the gap remained pretty much stable over the decades. This is especially true for PhDs (*Chart III.4*). In fact, in all areas of PhDs except engineering, the proportion of U.S. citizens or permanent residents[2] is significantly higher than foreigners (temporary visa holders).

Chart III.4

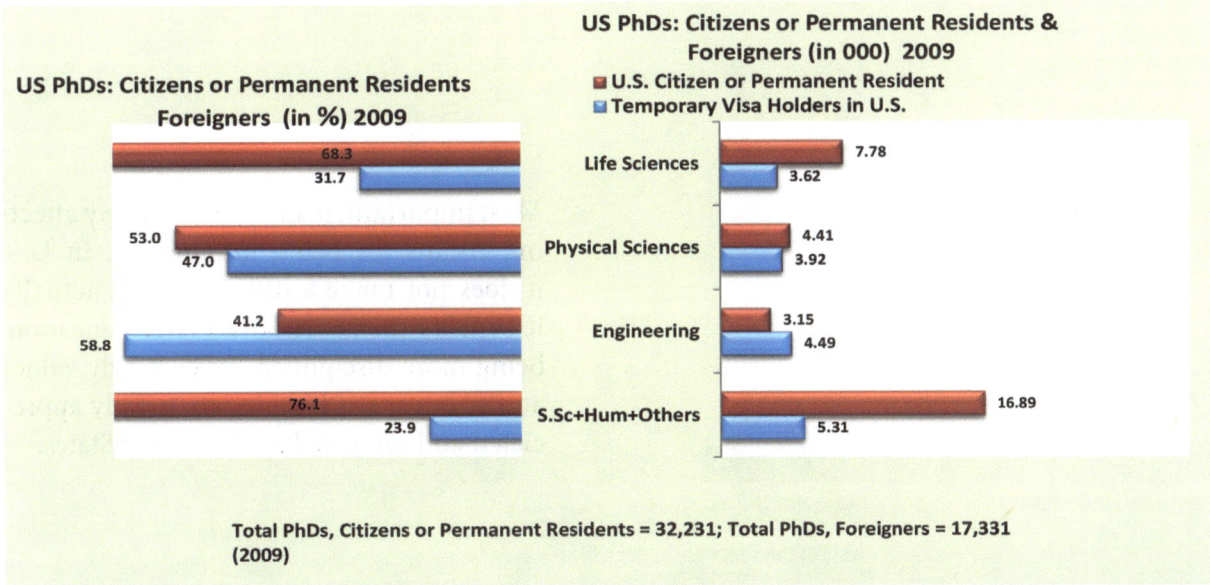

There have been several studies on earnings of domestic born and immigrants in both Canada and the United States, using various methodologies and set of data. All unequivocally show that immigrants have done far better in the United States than in Canada, even though immigrants did not have so much higher educational advantage in U.S. as they have in Canada.

For example, according to a recent Pew research[3] Asian American immigrants have 22% higher income than whites. In Canada, on the other hand, immigrants (Asian immigrants who are the dominant group) earn 15% less than Canadian born and the gap has been increasing over time.[4]

---

2   Note: U.S. PhDs numbers represent award of doctoral degrees in the country. One can be foreign born, but the education is completed in the United States. In Canada, on the other hand, more than 45% of total PhDs are immigrants who obtained degrees in their home land.

3   Pew Research Center (June 2012) *The Rise of Asian Americans* www.pewsocialtrends.org. Based on survey of 3,511 Asian Americans and U.S. Census Bureau data.

4   Statistics Canada (2009) *Canadian Immigrant Labour Market: Analysis of Quality of Employment* by Jason Gilmore, Catalogue no. 71-606-X, no. 5.

This is at the top that immigrants have 200% more higher education than Canadian born (see *Chart III.2*). In U.S., Asian immigrants have 58% higher educational advantage as compared to Whites.

Chart III.5

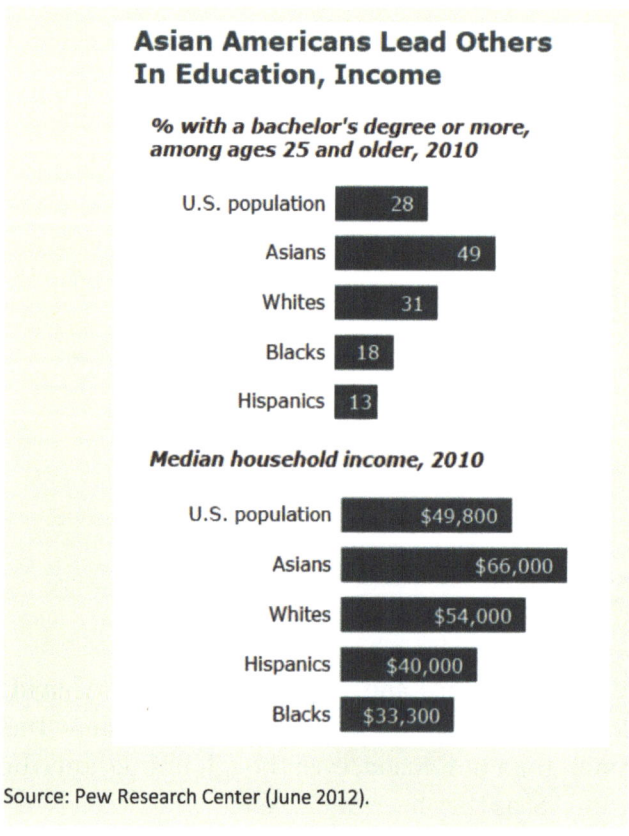

Source: Pew Research Center (June 2012).

Most important, instead of negatively affecting Asians for being immigrants, in U.S. it does not make a difference and actually it benefits them. Asians' better education, being more disciplined, strict family values and stronger work ethics are greatly appreciated and rewarded in the United States.

Chart III.6

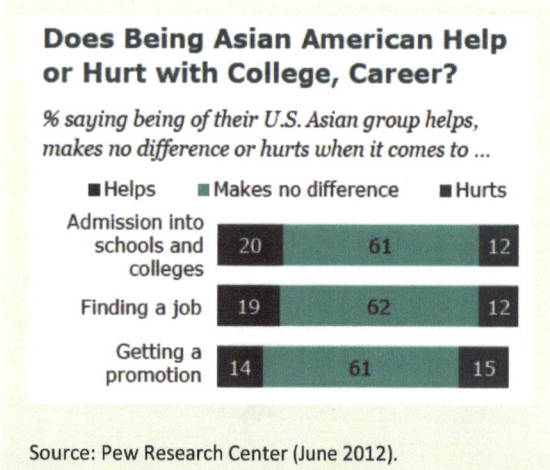

Source: Pew Research Center (June 2012).

One estimate (*Chart III.7*) using a more refined methodology and controlling the difference of age, language, region of origin and residence[5] found that the gap in earnings (year 2005) between domestic born and new immigrants was as high as 66% for women and 63% for men in Canada as compared to 35% for men and 44% for women in the United States.

Chart III.7

Adjusted*weekly wages of university-educated new immigrants relative to the domestic-born

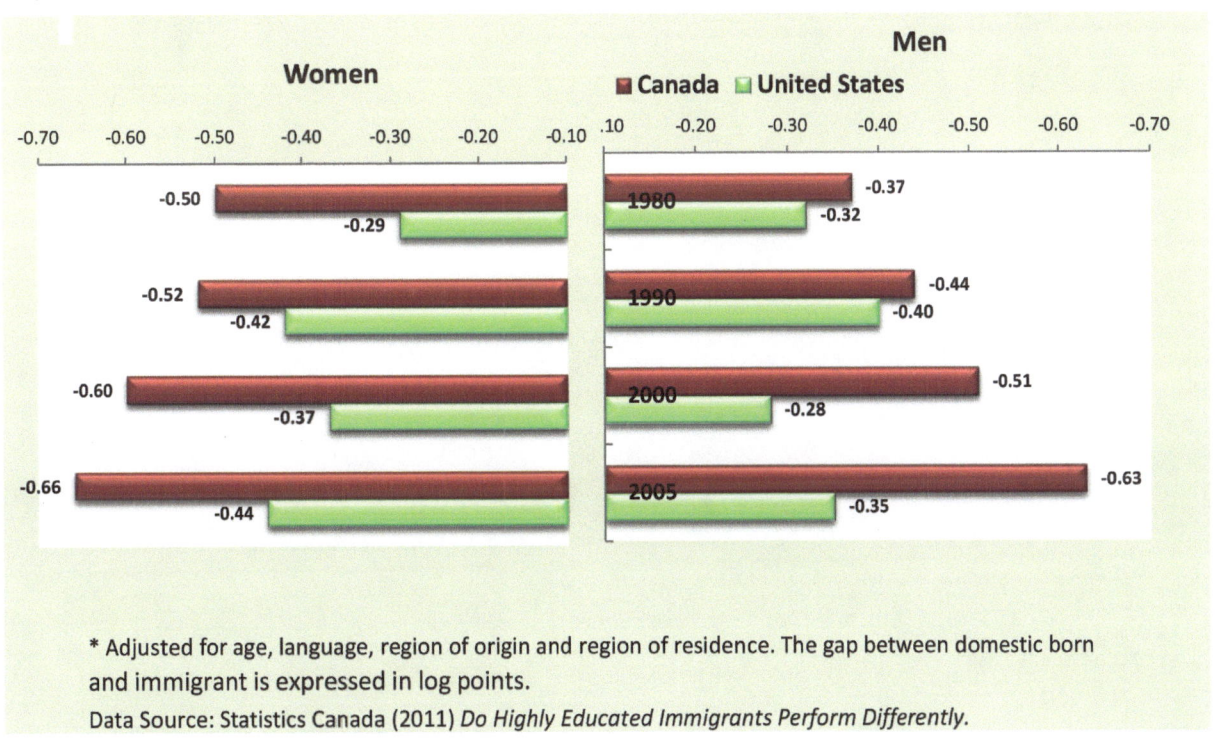

* Adjusted for age, language, region of origin and region of residence. The gap between domestic born and immigrant is expressed in log points.
Data Source: Statistics Canada (2011) *Do Highly Educated Immigrants Perform Differently.*

---

5   Statistics Canada (2011) *Do Highly Educated Immigrants Perform Differently* (Table 7).

Another estimate (*Chart III.8*)[6] measures the gap in earnings of domestic born and immigrants as ratios. It shows that for each dollar that domestic born earn (in 2001-05), immigrant men in Canada made 58 cents and women, 64 cents as compared to immigrant men in U.S. making 82 cents and women, 85 cents.

Chart III.8

Average weekly wages of university graduates, Ratio: Domestic Born to Immigrants (5-11 years since migration)*

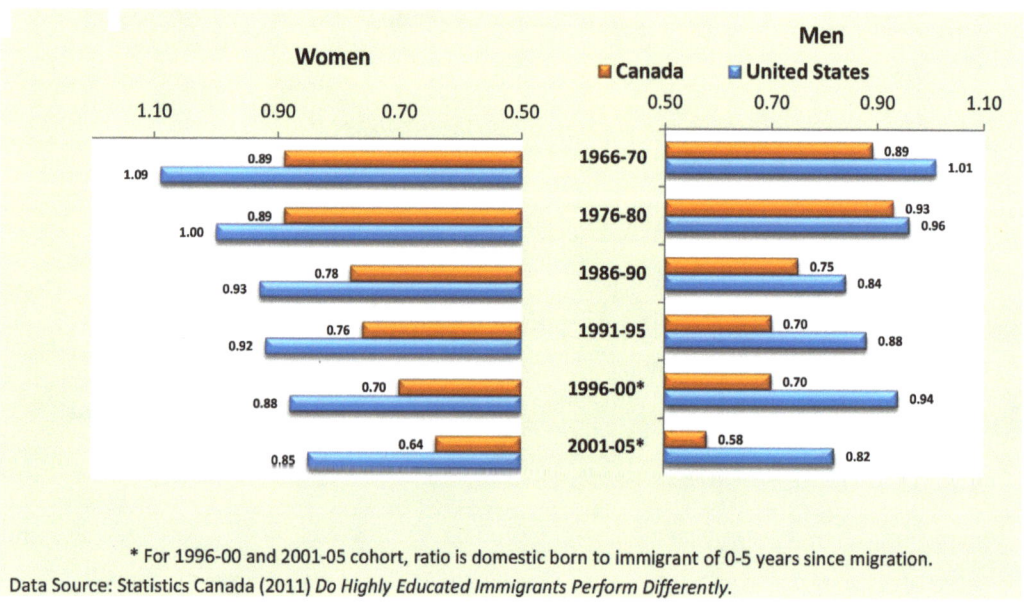

* For 1996-00 and 2001-05 cohort, ratio is domestic born to immigrant of 0-5 years since migration.
Data Source: Statistics Canada (2011) *Do Highly Educated Immigrants Perform Differently.*

---

6   Statistics Canada (2011) *Do Highly Educated Immigrants Perform Differently* (Table 7).

Over-qualification

According to an international comparison (2003),[7] overqualified — qualification exceeds the requirement to perform an assigned job — graduates (that include all level of education) were 26% in Canada as compared to 14.2% in the United States and 7.8% in OECD (not shown here).

Chart III.9

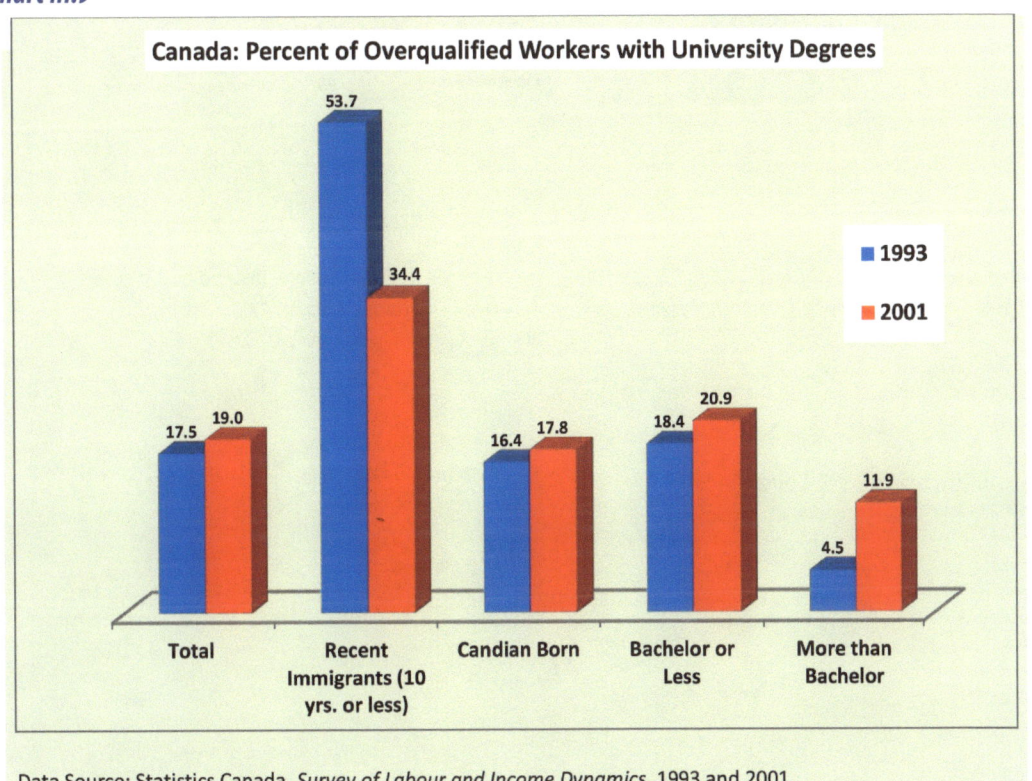

Canada: Percent of Overqualified Workers with University Degrees

Data Source: Statistics Canada, *Survey of Labour and Income Dynamics,* 1993 and 2001.

A detailed breakdown of overqualified workers with university degrees for Canada is given in *Chart III.9.* With the exception of immigrants, percentage of overqualified workers increased from 1993 to 2001 and especially those with post graduate degrees. However, within immigrants, over qualification is twice high as compared to Canadian born: 34.4% vs. 17.8% in 2001.

Within postgraduate degree holders, Statistics Canada found (based on graduates of 1990 who were surveyed in 1995) that 63% of men and 56% of women were overqualified with Master's degree

---

7   Human Resources Development Canada (2003) *How Canada Stacks Up: The Quality of Work — An International Perspective* by Richard Brisbois.

(Table 7, p.18)[8]; and 43.5% of men and 40% of women were overqualified with PhDs degree (Table 8, p. 19).

Chart III.10

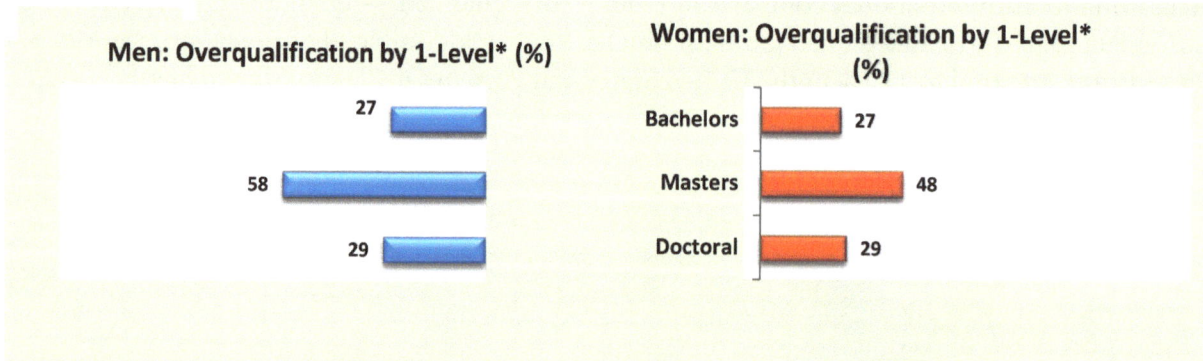

*1-Level implies that job requires Master instead of PhD, Bachelor instead of Master and College instead of Bachelor. Data Source: Statistics Canada *Education Quarterly Review*, 2000, Vol. 7, No. 1– Catalogue no. 81-003.

Chart III.11

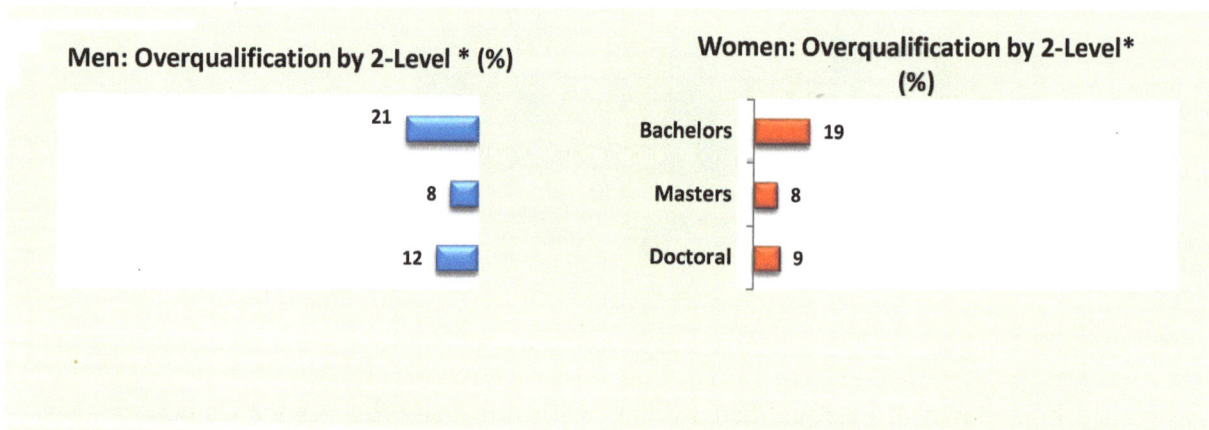

*2-Level implies that job requires Bachelor instead of PhD, College instead of Master and Diploma instead of Bachelor. Data Source: Statistics Canada *Education Quarterly Review*, 2000, Vol. 7, No. 1– Catalogue no. 81-003.

The severity of the over qualification is presented in Charts *III.10* and *III.11*. For example, 58% of men (and 48% of women) with Masters were employed in jobs that required Bachelor degree; while

---

8   Stat can (Nov. 2000) "Overqualified? Recent graduates and the needs of their employers," *Education Quarterly Review*, Vol. 7, no. 1 http://www.statcan.gc.ca/pub/81-003-x/81-003-x2000001-eng.pdf

29% of both men and women with PhDs actually needed Master's degree to do their jobs. The worse scenario (*Chart III.11*) is that 12% of men and 9% of women with PhDs are working on those jobs that needed only Bachelor degree.

According to a federal immigration study,[9] *Who Drives a Taxi in Canada* based on a survey of 50,101 cabbies last year found that half are immigrants and two hundreds are doctors or PhDs, compared with just 55 of their Canadian-born counterparts. 5.4% held a Master degree, compared to 1% of Canadian cabbies. And 14% of immigrant cabbies had a Bachelor degree, as compared to about 4% of Canadian-born. Bottom line: It is no longer an urban myth; 0.8% of immigrant PhDs and even 0.22% of Canadian-born cabbies are PhDs.

The percentage of PhD graduates who get an academic position has been falling and is now estimated to be less than 20% in Canada, according to panelists in annual Canadian Science Policy Conference , held in Ottawa mid-November, 2011.[10]

---

[9] The Globe and Mail (May 10, 2012) "Overqualified immigrants really are driving taxis in Canada" http://www.theglobeandmail.com/commentary/editorials/overqualified-immigrants-really-are-driving-taxis-in-canada/article4106352/

[10] Reported in University Affairs by Léo Charbonneau http://www.universityaffairs.ca/is-canada-producing-too-many-Ph.Ds..aspx .

Although we do not have detailed breakdown, but U.S. data for Public Universities which have close similarities to Canadian Universities (*Chart III.12*) provide grim picture. There is 31% decrease in full time tenured positions over a decade, while full time non-tenured and part time positions increased by 21% and 31%, respectively. One would expect worse academic prospects for PhDs in Canada.

Chart III.12

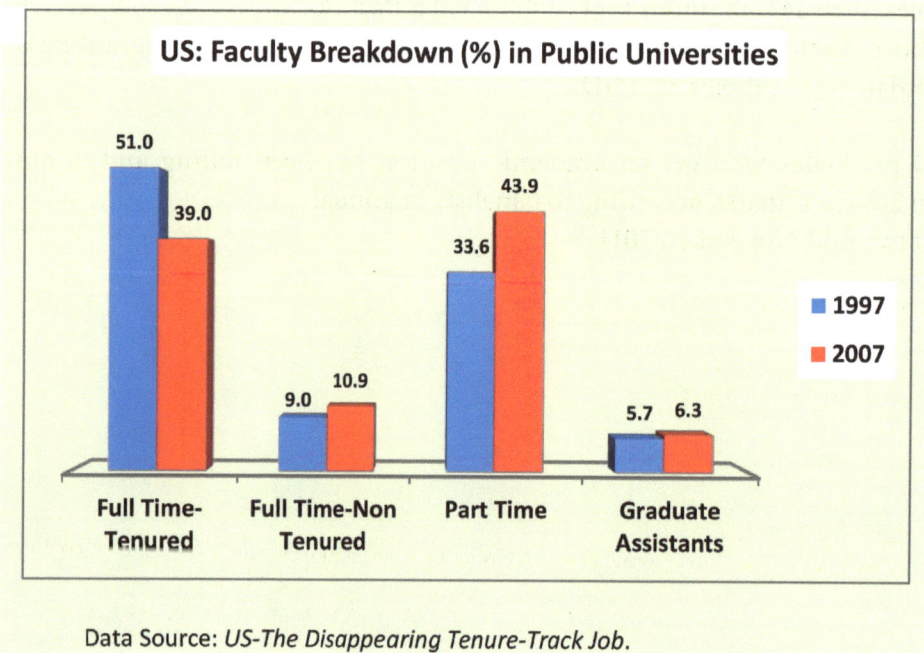

Data Source: *US-The Disappearing Tenure-Track Job.*

In fact, according to The Royal Society of Canada, "just 4 per cent of those who obtain a higher degree in science, gain a permanent academic research post, and less than half of 1 per cent end up as professors."[11]

Bleak job prospects for PhDs in Canada are further reinforced by the fact that private sectors hire only 4% of PhDs due to low R&D need and resource based nature of Canadian economy. It is the academia, which hires the bulk, 87% of PhDs,[12] but where job prospects are dwindling each coming year due to continued budget cuts, especially in higher education. In contrast, U.S. private sectors (business, industry and other organizations) employ 42% of PhDs, government, 7%, and academia, 51%.[13]

---

[11]   Phil Baty: http://www.timeshighereducation.co.uk/story.asp?storycode=420262

[12]   Statistics Canada (2005) *Survey of Earned Doctorates: A Profile of Doctoral Degree Recipients* by Tomasz Gluszynski and Valerie Peters, Catalogue no. 81-595-MIE — No. 032

[13]   NSF/NIH/U.S.ED/U.S.DA/NEH/NASA (2010) *Survey of Earned Doctorates* (2009).

Chapter IV: Reasons for Lower Economic Return of PhDs

Natural resources could be an impediment in moving towards an innovative and technologically advanced economy. It may make a nation lethargic, short-sighted and dependent on easy earning through sale of raw and primary inputs, especially when a large part of emerging and growing economies have hunger to buy raw materials.

Chart IV.1

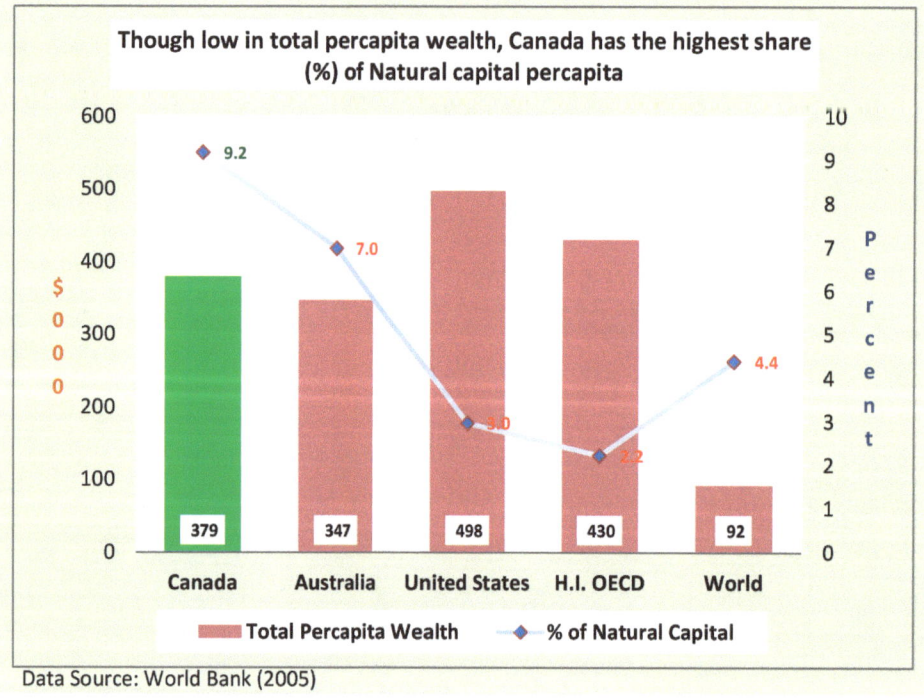

Data Source: World Bank (2005)

Canada has the highest share of natural capital on per capita basis at 9.2% (*Chart IV.1*). The share is more than 3 times higher than the United States and more than 4 times greater than the high income OECD countries. It is also 31.4% higher than Australia, another resource rich developed country.

Chart IV.2

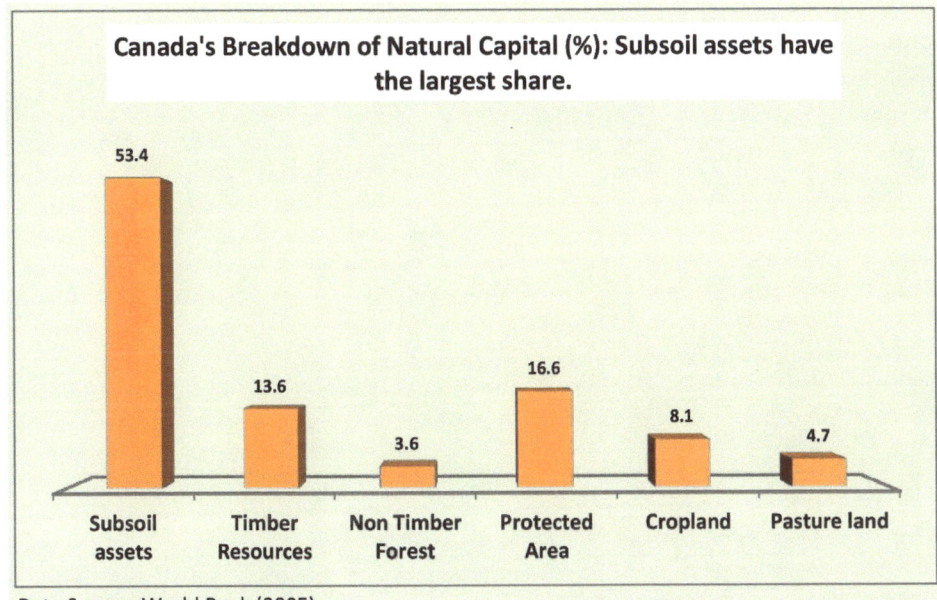

Canada's Breakdown of Natural Capital (%): Subsoil assets have the largest share.

53.4 — Subsoil assets
13.6 — Timber Resources
3.6 — Non Timber Forest
16.6 — Protected Area
8.1 — Cropland
4.7 — Pasture land

Data Source: World Bank (2005)

Subsoil assets (energy and minerals) at 53.4% is the main source of Canada's natural wealth (*Chart IV.2*), followed by forestry resources (17.2%).

However, as a result of low intangible and produced capitals (which are generated from research and value added activities), Canada's per capita total wealth is low as compared to United States and high income OECD countries (*Chart IV.1*).[1]

---

1   Estimated and converted into graph from World Bank (2005): *Where Is the Wealth of Nations? Measuring Capital for the XXI Century*, Conference Edition, 2005, Appendix 2 Country Level Wealth Estimates, 2000, p. 171-74; and World Bank, *Wealth Estimates by Country*, 2000. http://web.worldbank.org/WBSITE/EXTERNAL/TOPICS/ENVIRONMENT/EX-TEEI/0,,contentMDK:20487828~menuPK:1187788~pagePK:148956~piPK:216618~theSitePK:408050,00.html

Chart IV.3

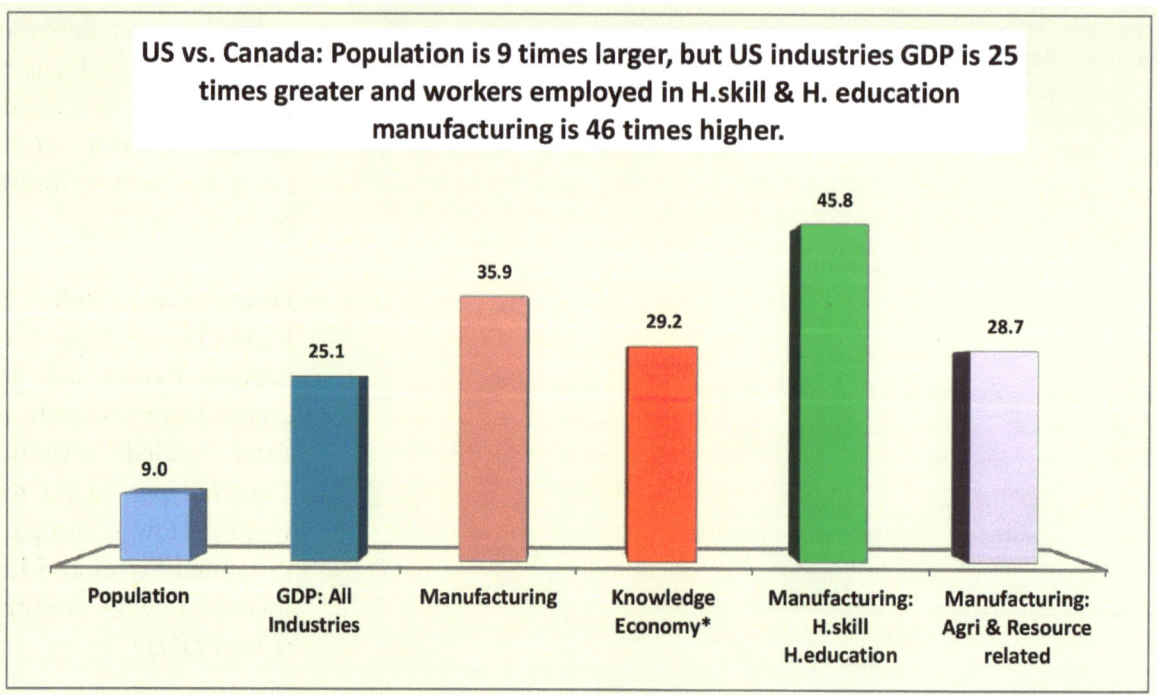

US vs. Canada: Population is 9 times larger, but US industries GDP is 25 times greater and workers employed in H.skill & H. education manufacturing is 46 times higher.

* Knowledge economy includes information, cultural industries, finance, banking, insurance, scientific, technical, educational, health care, arts & entertainment.

Although population of U.S. is only nine times larger than Canada, but in dollar value, it's GDP for all industries is 25 times higher and knowledge economy is 29 times greater. And within manufacturing, activities that require high skill and high education, the figure is 46 times higher in U.S. as compared to Canada (*Chart 1V.3*).[2] This provides ample job opportunities and economic growth for PhDs in U.S. as compared to Canada.

---

2   Statistics Canada (June 2010) *Catalogue no. 15-001-X*. Estimated (3 years: 2007, 2008, 2009 average in 2002 $B) and converted into graph from Canada Gross domestic product at basic prices, overview — Annual); and Bureau of Economic Analysis (May 2010) *Industry Economic Accounts*. Estimated (3 years: 2006, 2007, 2008 average in $B) and converted into graph from Gross-Domestic-Product-by-Industry Accounts.

Overall, knowledge economy accounts for 41% in Canada (*Chart IV.4*) as compared to 48% in United States with its 29 times larger economy (*Chart IV.5*). Within manufacturing sector in Canada, high skill and high education accounts for 43%, while resource related production activities, 57%.

Chart IV.4

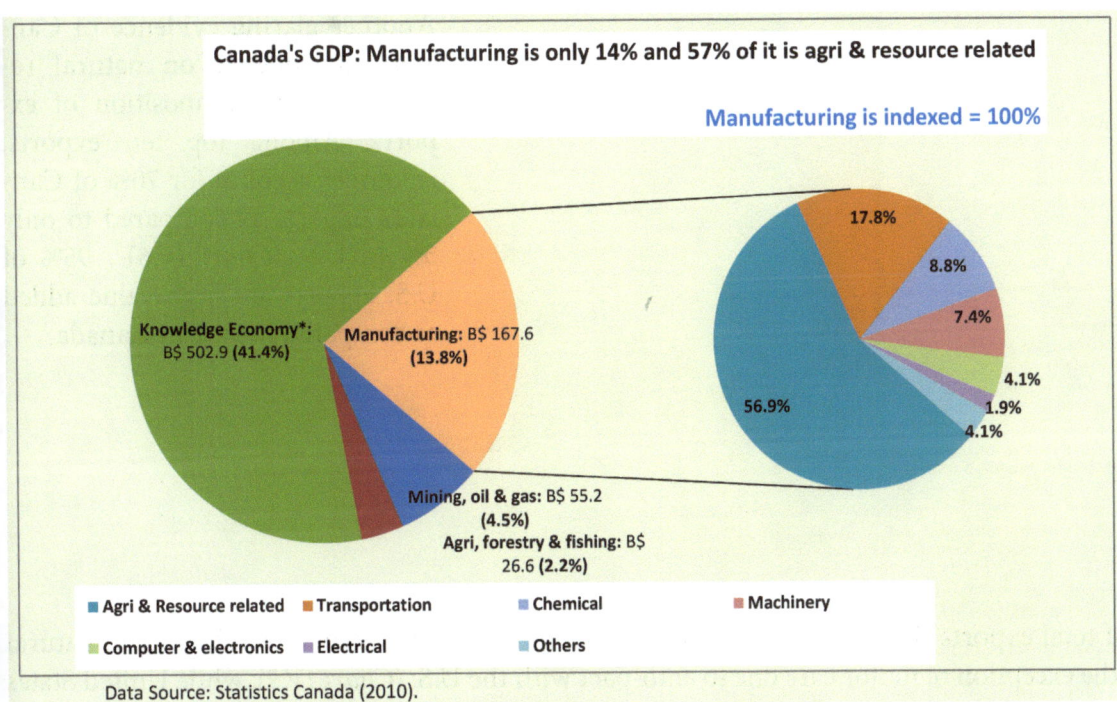

Canada's GDP: Manufacturing is only 14% and 57% of it is agri & resource related

Manufacturing is indexed = 100%

Data Source: Statistics Canada (2010).

Chart IV.5

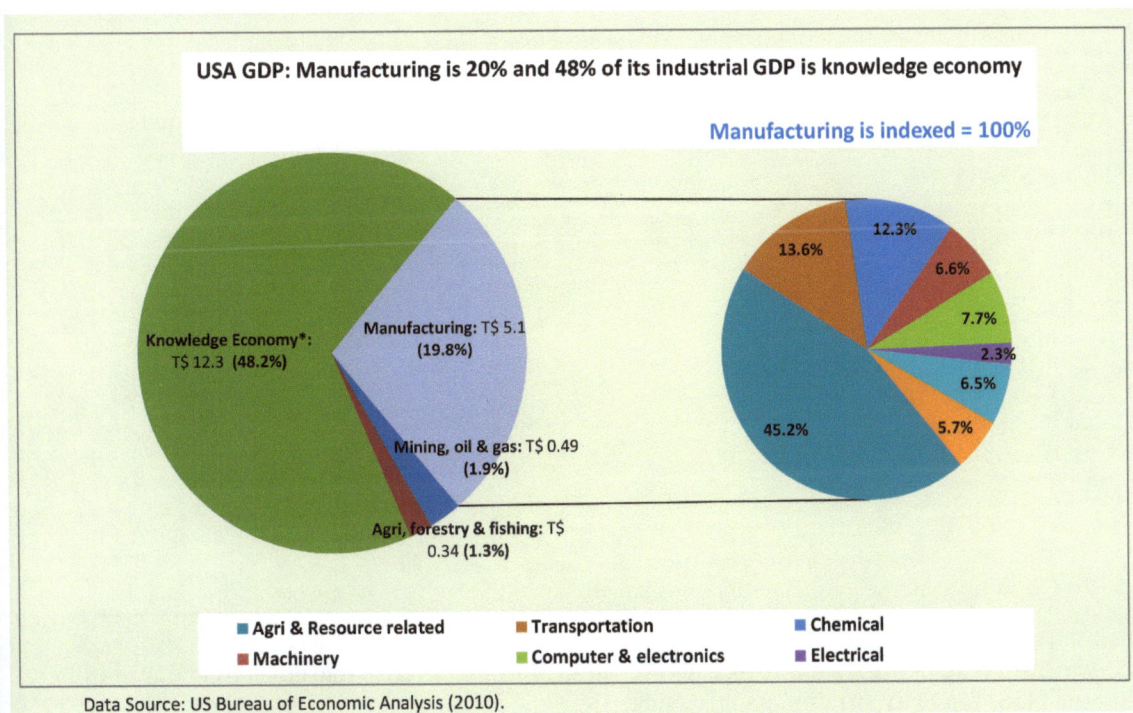

USA GDP: Manufacturing is 20% and 48% of its industrial GDP is knowledge economy

Manufacturing is indexed = 100%

Data Source: US Bureau of Economic Analysis (2010).

Chart IV.6

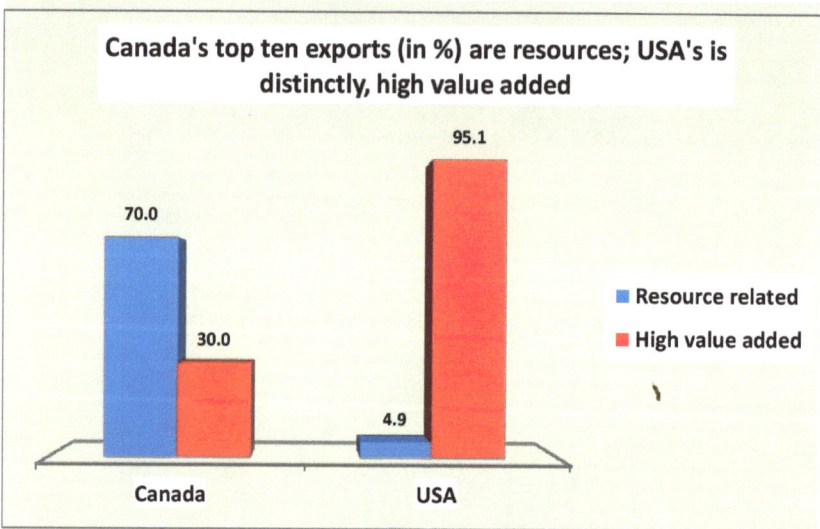

Another glaring evidence of Canada's dependence on natural resources is its composition of exports. Among top ten exports, resources account for 70% of Canada's exports as compared to only 5% in U.S. (*Chart IV.6*)[3]: 95% of U.S. exports are high value added as compared to 30% in Canada.

Data Source: UN Comtrade (various years).

A breakdown of total exports shows that Canada's top ten exports are dominated by oil, gas and natural resources with the exception of motor cars due to auto-pact with the U.S. (*Chart IV.7*), while United States top ten exports are clearly high value added, petro products, electronics etc. (Chart *IV.8*)

3   *UN Comtrade.* Estimated (3 years: 2007, 2008, 2009 average in $B) and converted into graph from Canada Top 10 Export Commodities and U.S. Top 10 Export Commodities, Table 3.

Chart IV.7

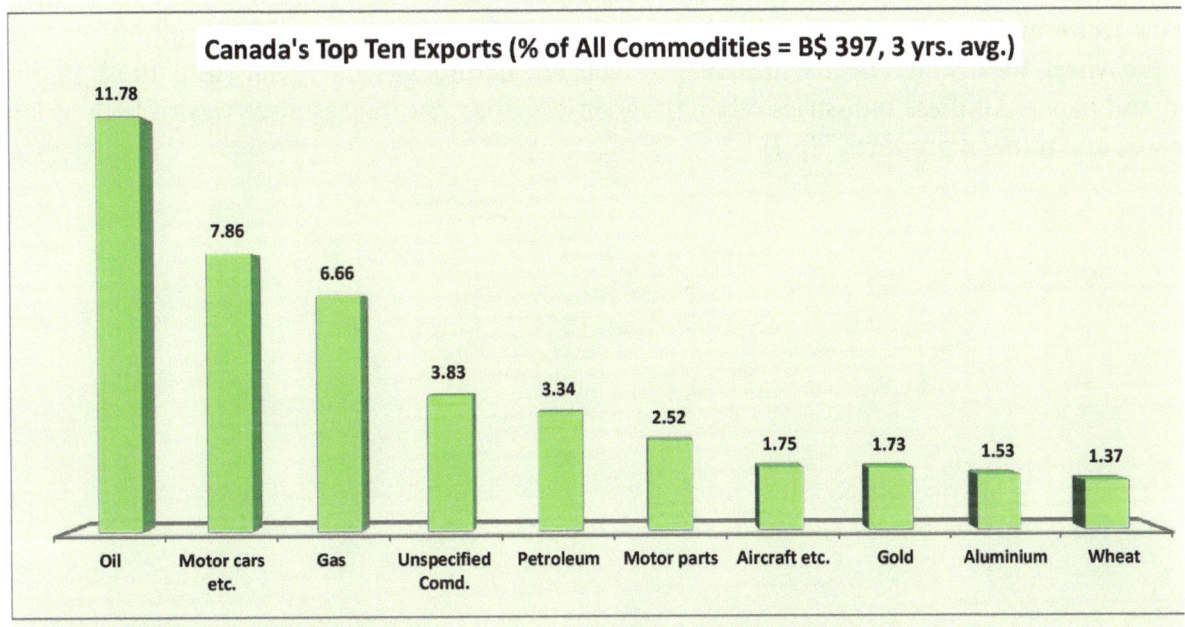

Canada's Top Ten Exports (% of All Commodities = B$ 397, 3 yrs. avg.)

Oil	11.78
Motor cars etc.	7.86
Gas	6.66
Unspecified Comd.	3.83
Petroleum	3.34
Motor parts	2.52
Aircraft etc.	1.75
Gold	1.73
Aluminium	1.53
Wheat	1.37

Data Source: UN Comtrade (various years).

Chart IV.8

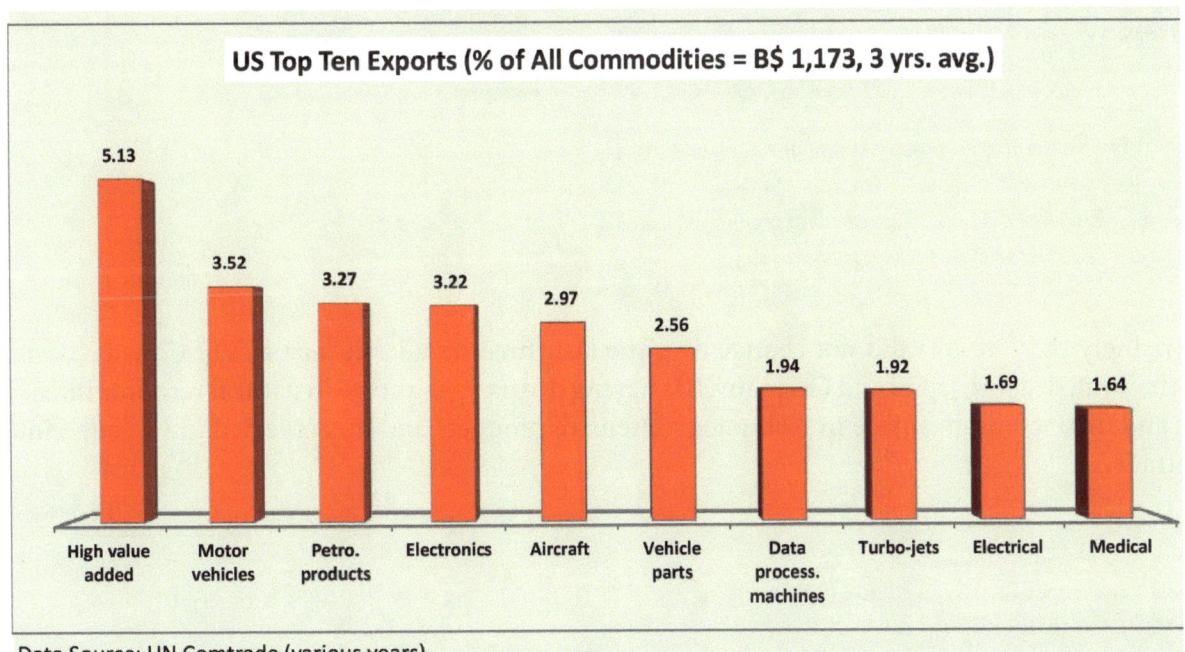

US Top Ten Exports (% of All Commodities = B$ 1,173, 3 yrs. avg.)

High value added	5.13
Motor vehicles	3.52
Petro. products	3.27
Electronics	3.22
Aircraft	2.97
Vehicle parts	2.56
Data process. machines	1.94
Turbo-jets	1.92
Electrical	1.69
Medical	1.64

Data Source: UN Comtrade (various years).

A recent study[4] using more comprehensive method of measuring the strength of a country in commodity exports, Revealed Comparative Advantage index concludes: "Our strengths are highly concentrated in the primary sector and in the industries that process raw materials. These include agricultural and food products like wheat, meat, and oilseeds; mineral products like natural gas and metals; and forest products like wood and paper. All these industries rely heavily on Canada's natural resource wealth such as land, water, forests, and mineral products." (p.2).

Chart IV.9

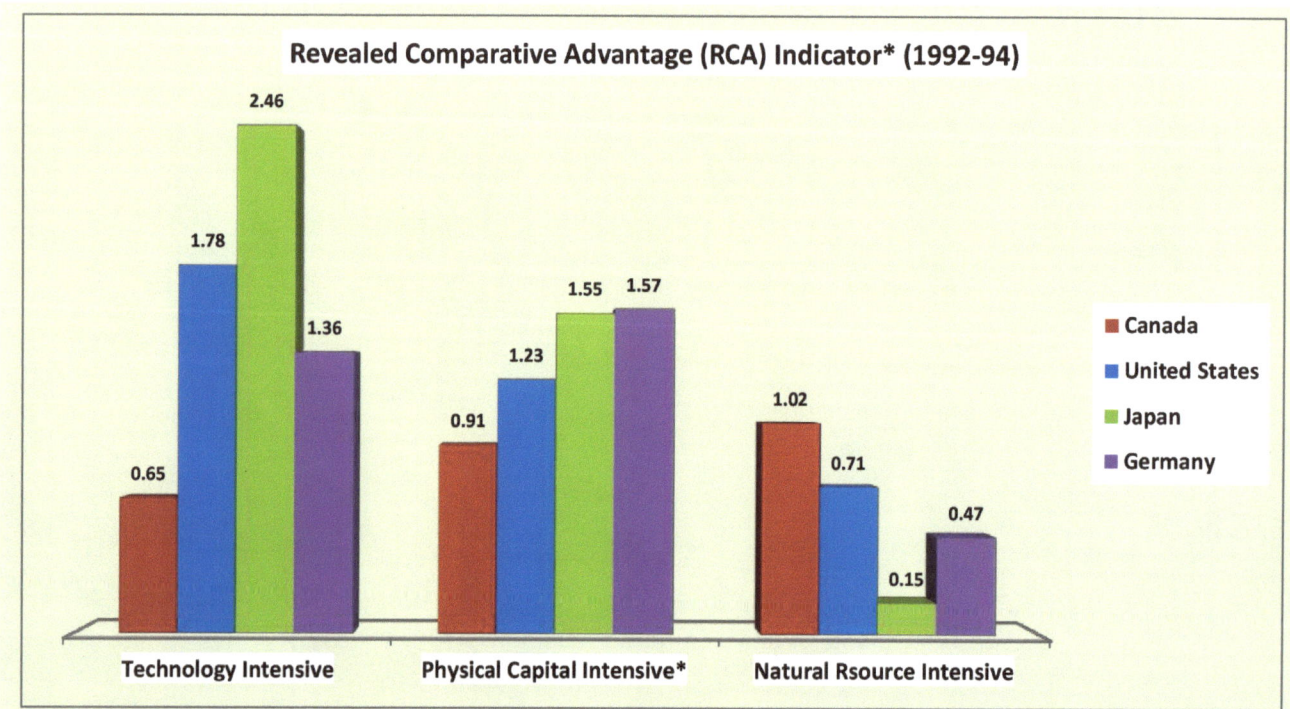

Revealed Comparative Advantage (RCA) Indicator* (1992-94)

RCA Indicator = Greater than 1 indicates Comparative Advantage; less than 1 indicates comparative Disadvantage.
RCA Indicator is basically the same for the year 1980-82.
*Physical captial intensive group is composed of chemicals, iron & steel, nonferrous metals and machinery.
Data Source: The Conference Board of Canada (1996).

Not surprisingly those results did not change over the last three decades (*Chart IV.9*).[5] Canada as compared to the United States, Japan and Germany, has having distinct advantage in natural resource intensive products and distinct disadvantage in technology intensive products and it is reflected in Canada's international trade.

---

4   The Conference Board of Canada (2012) *Adding Value to Trade: Moving Beyond Being Hewers of Wood* by Kristelle Audet and Michael Burt.

5   The Conference Board of Canada (1996) *Performance and Potential* (Mahmood Iqbal, author of the chapter).

Dominance of natural resources in Canadian economy is again reflected in the fluctuation of Canadian $ against the U.S. $. Canadian $ moves in close harmony with the price of its raw natural resources (*Chart IV.10*).

Chart IV.10

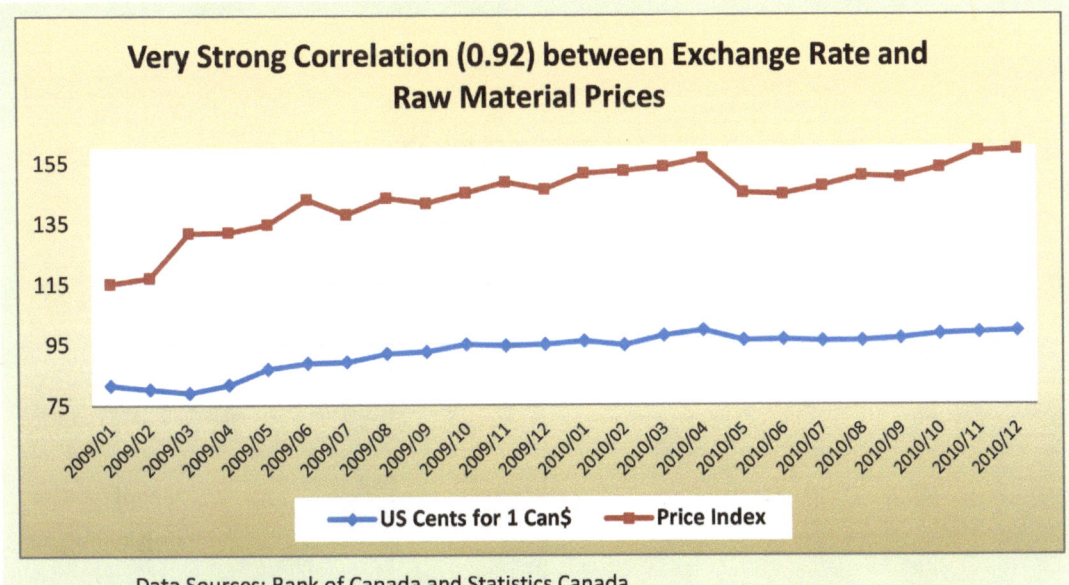

Data Sources: Bank of Canada and Statistics Canada.

Chart IV.11

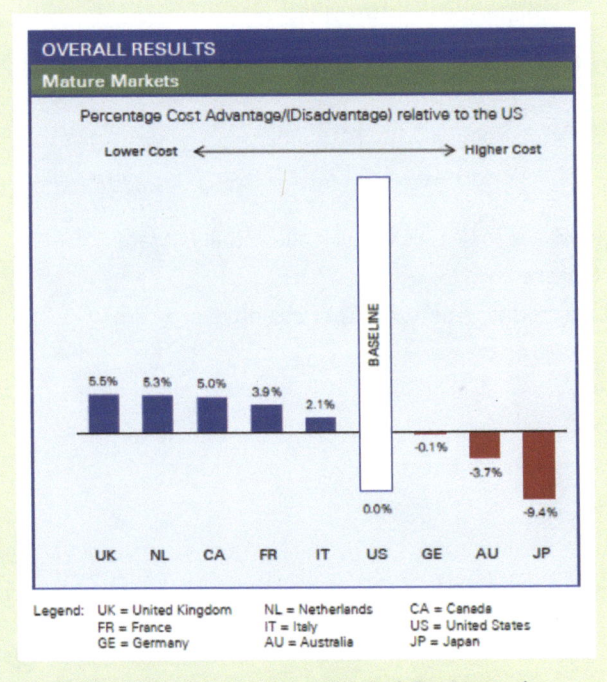

Legend: UK = United Kingdom   NL = Netherlands   CA = Canada
        FR = France   IT = Italy   US = United States
        GE = Germany   AU = Australia   JP = Japan

Note: The four largest US metro areas—New York City, Los Angeles, Chicago, and Dallas-Fort Worth—form the US baseline against which costs for major cities in other countries are compared.
Data Source: KPMG (2012) *Competitive Alternatives*, p. ii.

Canada's dismal performance in knowledge related and skilled manufacturing activities can be observed in a broader competitive study conducted by the KPMG each year.[6] Based on a total cost comparison of 19 business operations in leading competing jurisdictions, Canada has 5% cost advantage over U.S. (*Chart IV.11*)

_____

6   KPMG (2012) *Competitive Alternatives*. http://www.competitivealternatives.com/download/default.aspx

Also (*Chart IV.12*) all income taxes paid by business is 89.5% lower for manufacturing and 156% lower for R&D companies in Canada as compared to the United States. Still business investment outside oil, gas, forestry and natural resource extraction is limited in Canada. And so are the employment opportunities for highly educated personals in knowledge intensive manufacturing and R&D industries.

Chart IV.12

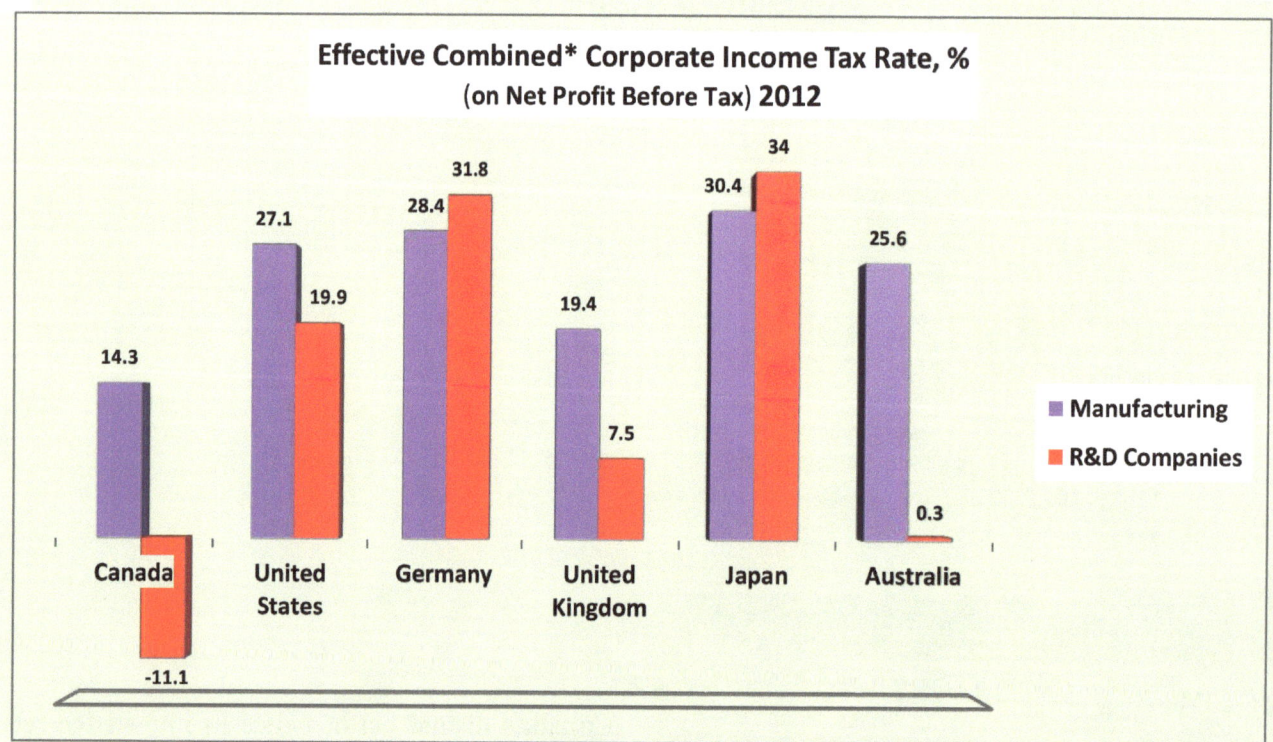

Effective Combined* Corporate Income Tax Rate, %
(on Net Profit Before Tax) 2012

*Combined corporate income tax rate includes federal, regional and local taxes. This is the actual tax rate paid by companies after taking account various deductions and credits.
Note: Negative rate is the result of refundable R&D income tax credits, grants, or other incentive programs.
Data Source: KPMG (2012) *Competitive Alternatives*.

Expenditure on research and development is an effective barometer of measuring the strength and commitment of a country towards invention, innovation and adopting new technologies in fast changing and competitive production and learning environment. Not surprisingly, following the previous pattern of production and exports of commodities, Canada is basically close to the bottom of competing OECD countries in R&D (*Chart IV.13*). Canada's gross expenditure on R&D as a percentage of its GDP is 1.92 as compared to Finland's 3.92, United States' 2.9 and OECD average of 2.4. Canada is also behind Australia, which is basically a resource based economy.

Chart IV.13

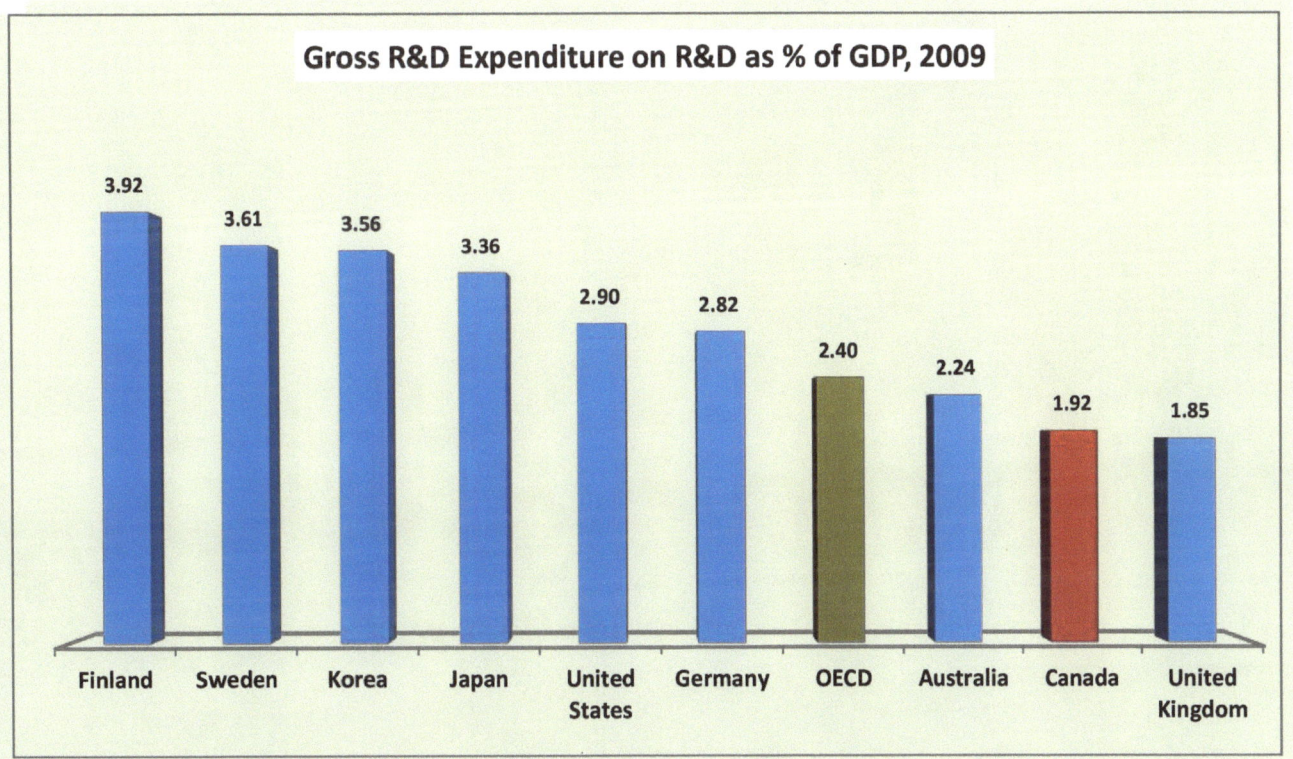

Data Source: OECD (2012) *Main Science and Technology Indicators.*

And when it comes to business expenditure on R&D, Canada is at the bottom (*Chart IV.14*). As a percentage of its GDP, it is only 0.99 as compared to Finland's 2.81, United States' 1.93 and Australia's 1.3. "Canada's (BERD) ranking has been essentially unchanged over the past 25 years despite repeated calls and policy initiatives aimed at stimulating much greater R&D effort by Canadian businesses."(p. 56)[7]

Chart IV.14

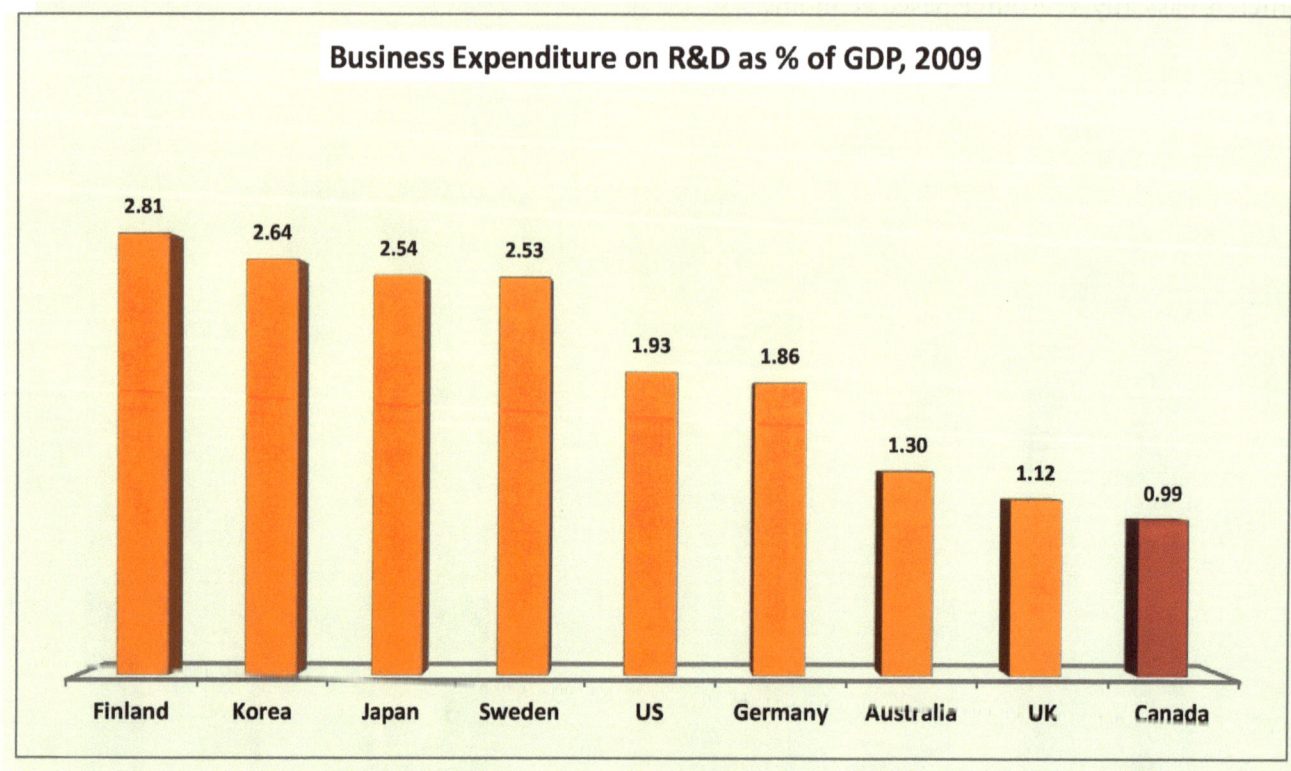

Data Source: OECD (2012) *Main Science and Technology Indicators.*

---

7   Council of Canadian Academies (2009) *Innovation and Business Strategy: Why Canada Falls Short*, Ottawa.

Chart IV.15

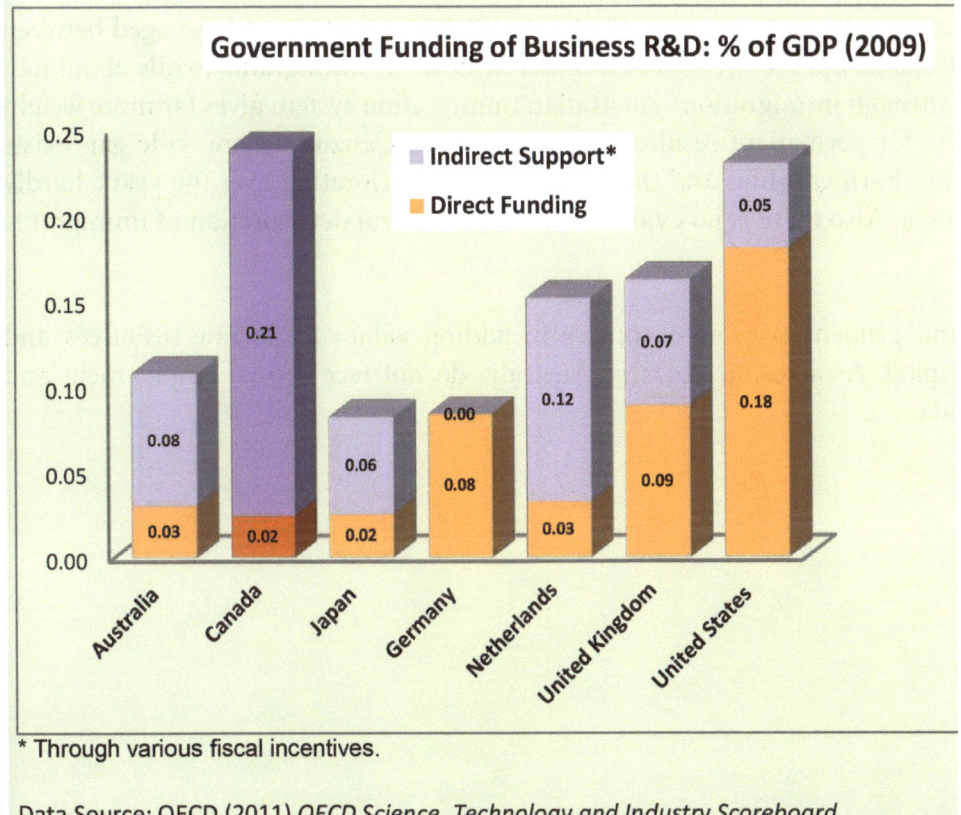

Government Funding of Business R&D: % of GDP (2009)

* Through various fiscal incentives.

Data Source: OECD (2011) *OECD Science, Technology and Industry Scoreboard.*

The above quote is buttressed by *Chart IV.15*. Canada has always been at the top among OECD countries in R&D related incentives (largely tax credits and deductions). However, in Canadian business calculation these tax benefits were not sufficient enough to engage in greater R&D activities, after adjusting risks with the rate of return; and by extension their intention to hire more PhDs.

According to World Economic Forum,[8] this year Canada's global competitiveness ranking is 14th, even behind Qatar and Taiwan. The position has been slipping each recent years. It was 10th in 2010. The main reason for this sliding ranking is clear: poor performance in innovation (22nd) and lack of business sophistication (26th). Areas where higher education can play key role in uplifting competitive ranking but its importance has been undermined due to dominance of the resource sector.

Bottom line: In an economic environment where country is richly endowed with natural resources (for which world is hungry, especially the emerging economies in Asia), and Canada can harness, extract and sell them without much effort and adding higher value, Canadian economy does not find much value of employing highly educated graduates: Masters and especially PhDs. Those graduates do not have much alternative than to be un-or under-employed or work in industries and institutions where their education is not needed, in other words, they are over-qualified.

---

8   World Economic Forum (2012): *The Global Competitiveness Report, 2012-2013*, Geneva.

Australia is another advanced resource rich country like Canada, but size of its natural wealth is significantly lower. Its omposition of natural wealth is also different. Austalia's export of natural resources is more processing rather than raw. It produces more PhDs per 100,000 population (those aged between 25 and 29)[9] as compared to Canada, but receives small number of PhDs as immigrants (while about half of Canada's total PhDs come through immigration). Australian immigration system gives far more weight to skill than higher education for permanent residency. In contrast to Canada, where wide gap exists between immigrants and native born earnings and the gap has been deteriorating over the years, hardly such disparity exists in Australia. Also there is no evidence of inter temporal deterioration of immigrants earning in Australia.[10]

Australia took far-sighted and prudent economic policies in adding values to its raw resources and employment of its human capital. As a result, PhDs in Australia do not face dismal employment and earning prospects as in Canada.

[9]   Internationally comparable data are available only for PhDs in age group of 25-29. Source: OECD (2009) *Education at a Glance 2009.*

[10]   Andrew Clarkey and Mikal Skuterudz (2012) *Why Do Immigrant Workers in Australia Perform Better Than in Canada? Is It the Immigrants or Their Labour Markets?* http://arts.uwaterloo.ca/~skuterud/Mikal_Skuterud/Research_files/ clarke_skuterud_census.pdf

Chapter V: Issues and Future Challenges

The most disturbing aspect of PhDs dismal prospect is that there is already little opportunity for them outside academia; and those who work for governments as bureaucrats and policy makers are humiliated and bypassed by politicians who often hold the equivalent of a bachelor degree and mediocre work experience. And the sad thing is that constitutionally it appears that decision making power rests solely with politicians (instead of arm's length institutions, independent experts and bureaucrats) even in cases where decisions could have significant long-term negative implications on country's future. And politicians know very well how to squeeze the system for their own short-term goal of being elected.

Debacle of the long-form Census is a classic case in recent years,[1] for which the Chief Statistician had to resign while the Minister made disingenuous statements in the media to rationalize his decision. The decision was purely for ideological reasons. (And for ideology and belief, facts could be suffocating.) Anyone with an elementary understanding of Statistics knows that a survey (long-form Census was ditched in favour of Survey by the Minister) is not a substitute, because a Census is mandatory (not voluntary like surveys) with wide coverage of each segment of the society on random basis.

The decision was widely condemned by all national and international experts and users of Statscan publications. Discontinued long-form Census (in use for about 100 years) would have severe long-term negative implications. Canada is a vast country with ten provinces and two territories, each with its unique geography, diversity and socio-economic need. Detailed information of different aspects and segments of society are essential in determining equalization payment and goal of sustaining uniform standard in education, health, growth and prosperity in these jurisdictions.

Another recent case of autocratic power of a Minister was the cancellation of funding for KAIROS (an NGO) overseas projects, supported by CIDA for the last thirty five years.[2] In the House, International Development Minister denied that there was any political motivation. Later, an Access to Information

---

[1]   *The Globe and Mail* (July 21, 2010) "Canada's long-form census debate" http://www.theglobeandmail.com/news/politics/canadas-long-form-censU.S.-debate/article1387599/

[2]   *Macleans.ca* (February 28, 2011) http://www2.macleans.ca/2011/02/28/what-it-takes-to-get-fired/

request revealed that the funding was actually approved by CIDA's top officials' command chain; but the Minister rejected without a single sentence of reason, just inserting a hand-drawn word "NOT" in capital letter. (It was revealed later that the word NOT was inserted due to ideological reasons). Such is the power of a Minister without any experience and in depth understanding of the file. S/he can just snub senior bureaucrats' and experts' decision with a stroke of pen. It shows how much disrespect politicians have for highly educated people; and as a result their dismal prospect of being employed and prosper in governments.

It needs to be reiterated that the most disturbing aspect of Canada's constitution and political structure is that it bestows autocratic powers to a Minister (even with a minority government) to overrule experts who have no political axe to grind.

Some may say that the will of people, represented by elected politicians cannot be suppressed. But where is the will of people when less than 60% of electorates cast vote and a majority government is formed by 35% of popular vote. This implies that the present Harper government got a clear majority with only 21% (=60%*35%) of electorates vote. Moreover, none of these issues like ditching long-form census, employment insurance changes and pension reforms were ever raised during pre-election debates.

Demanding PhDs along with others, to be fluent in French (90% of whom use English as their working language) to hold senior positions in the federal government is another bottleneck in jobs and their career enhancement. Bilingualism deprives the country's 80% of the talent pool as often reflected in the quality and mediocrity of many *senior* bureaucrats (who got the position primarily due to French fluency), government officials and ministers. A regular manifestation is the quality of debates in the parliament.

However media, including reputable one like *Globe and Mail*[3] hail the ignorance and mediocrity of Canadian politicians. A veteran journalist very proudly wrote: "In a 2009 survey of Canada's 40th Parliament, the Ottawa-based Public Policy Forum found that 69.5%of MPs had university degrees, compared with 92.7% of members of Congress. ... Less educated legislators do a better job than more educated legislators – and Canada has the economy to prove it." Further, "California has the best-educated state legislators in the United States – and one of the worst economies. ...Further evidence of an inverse relationship between education and job performance – for legislators." The logical conclusion: the more illiterate a nation's political decision makers are, greater is its prospect for brighter economic future.

The journalist forgot to mention that when Greece and Italian economy tanked, power was taken away from legislators and given to technocrats who have PhDs and long work experiences in international financial institutions. In the Canadian context, it was the prudent economic policies, strict regulations and large budget surplus of previous governments (where meritocracy instead of ideology of ministers still used to play key role in decision making process) that saved present day Canada to have same ill fate as Europe.

---

3   *The Globe and Mail* (August 29, 2011) "Believe it or not: Less educated legislators do a better job" by Neil Reynolds http://www.theglobeandmail.com/news/opinions/opinion/believe-it-or-not-less-educated-legislators-do-a-better-job/article2143984/

Challenges

Facts presented in above sections clearly show that most of PhDs produced in Canada or those who immigrated are hardly needed. The job market for them is small and shrinking (as academia is the major employer and their budgets have been severely cut). It appears that Canadian PhDs must serve the bigger market in the United States or move overseas after graduation.

The logical question is that why does Canada produce PhDs far more in number than can be gainfully employed in the country. I believe it is more for psychological consolation. After all, Canada is in the league of advanced developed country; sitting next to the most technology savvy and knowledge rich country – U.S.A. It would be a matter of shame and humiliation if Canada also does not follow the course of other advanced countries when it comes to expenditure on higher education and production of highly educated people. Without realizing the fact that Canada is in some way a unique developed country due to its large dependence on raw natural resources for employment and economic wellbeing; and where PhDs are hardly needed.

The other question is how will you sustain the existing PhD programs in most Canadian universities on one hand and on the other, meeting the teaching need of increasing enrollment, especially of foreign students in undergraduate programs of science, engineering, business and economics. Solution: go on producing PhDs at full capacity, but employ them as part-timers or sessional instructors at salaries close to minimum wages without benefits. After all, financially strained universities are not in a position to hire them as regular faculty members and at the same time, there would be no shortage of PhDs when needed.

What is the future of higher education, especially PhDs in Canada? In the short run, PhDs will be produced basically to serve foreign markets, as brain drain to U.S. or to overseas; and to teach increasing number of foreign students in Canada. Already, about 50% of PhDs in sciences are foreign students.

In the long run, North American universities will setup campuses in the backyard of many Asian countries. It would be more cost effective. And this is already happening. Not only Harvard and MIT have campuses in Asia, Canada's York University's Schulich School of Business is setting up campus in India.[4] Dean of the school says "Why do corporations go abroad? To make a stronger base at home. To create a larger market. To reduce risk. If North America is declining in demand, we have to be in that part of the world."

There will be no shortage of qualified Professors to teach and do research in Asia as significant component of faculties in North American Universities are composed of immigrants and foreign nationals and they will not have much reservation in returning home once opportunities will arise there. As reported in the *Globe and Mail*,[5] by one account "about 100,000 [Indians] are said to have come back last year and the

---

4   *The Globe and Mail* (June 9, 2011) "Canadian education is going global" http://www.theglobeandmail.com/news/opinions/editorials/canadian-education-is-going-global/article2054292/

5   *The Globe and Mail* (May 15, 2012) "For many Indians, the land of opportunity is the land they're going back to" http://m.theglobeandmail.com/news/national/time-to-lead/for-many-indians-the-land-of-opportunity-is-the-land-theyre-going-back-to/article2431478/?service=mobile

number is growing" for better opportunity, security and family reasons. As in India, expatriates are returning to China – "drawn by more than just the natural pull of an economy that has grown by 9% or more every year since 2002. The many thousands of Chinese who went abroad for higher education are now being targeted by a massive government effort to bring back the country's best and brightest."[6]

Moreover, there will be no shortage of qualified students in Asia to be enrolled in PhD programs due to its immense young population, desire, prospect and respect for higher learning. Therefore, there is not much rationale of sustaining PhD programs in Canada in the long run.

Also, one cannot ignore the technological development in eLearning. *Coursera is* one example.[7] Started by the Stanford University and now joined by dozen other major universities, including Harvard and MIT; where best courses are offered on line from the best professors basically for free. This could drastically decrease the need, especially for new PhDs to teach undergraduate courses in the traditional face to face student-teacher environment.

However, it would be short sighted to ignore the other side of the coin: benefits of Canadian PhDs to the society and world at large. Higher education creates a more knowledgeable, civic and mature society with many unquantifiable non-economic benefits. Its advantages are multiplied in todays complicated, fast changing and challenging world. Canada basically provides indirect aid to many developing countries, whose students after graduation go back home to contribute to their countries. Further, many immigrants who become successful in carving better economic opportunities in Canada after their PhDs provide economic and non-pecuniary support to their families and friends back home.

Can anything be done?

The issue needs to be addressed from both demand and supply sides. Academia, government and private sector are main players in creating jobs on the demand side. Employment opportunities in universities are dwindling as stated earlier.[8] Size of governments is shrinking at all levels. In

---

6 *The Globe and Mail* (May 15, 2012) "China lures back its best." http://m.theglobeandmail.com/news/national/time-to-lead/china-lures-back-its-best/article2431479/?service=mobile

7 *The Globe and Mail* (July 19, 2012) "Online university for the masses!" by Margaret Wente http://www.theglobeandmail.com/commentary/online-university-for-the-masses/article4426073/

8 This study could have further dampening effect.

recent years, the federal government has shown many examples of antipathy towards contributions of experts in science and research — that's what most PhDs do — because research challenges politicians' ideology-based decisions. (This may also plague politicians' in provincial governments.)

A realistic and long-term solution for PhDs is creating an environment where private sector in Canada would find it more lucrative to hire them. The private sector in the United States hires eleven times more PhDs than Canada's. There is ample room for growth in their employment in this sector.

But why should the private sector do it? After all, Canadian businesses have not deviated from their century old traditional production and trade of raw and primary commodities even after billions of dollars were poured as various fiscal incentives by governments over the last three decades.

Moreover, given the fact that the world is becoming more competitive and the labour force more educated, Canadian private sector is content with the risk averse and short sighted traditional business practices. It appears that the sector has not yet reached the tipping point where it would find that the economic return from manufacturing and trade of high value-added and specialized technology-led products outweighs the profits generated from traditional resource-based economic activities.

On the supply side, funding and its allocation to higher education — Bachelors, Masters and Doctorates — would need to be reevaluated: which program brings highest economic return after adjusting for time, monetary and other costs. This too, is clearly not in favour of PhDs. Canada can continue pursuing its current path of producing PhDs with only the objective of having intrinsic benefits of a highly educated society. It could also serve the world by enabling foreign students to attain a PhD and emigrate after their graduation in order to accelerate the process of economic development in their home countries.[9] PhDs could also act as goodwill ambassadors, which may benefit Canada in the distant future.

---

9   A note of clarification: a significant number of PhDs from foreign countries come to Canada as immigrants to escape dismal economic prospect, war and political upheaval in their home countries. Recent immigration data of Indian and Chinese immigrants show that they started going back home as economic and political situation improve there. Moreover, many foreign students who come to Canada in various PhD programs, especially in Sciences, they plan to go back home after completing their education here.